A Brief History of the Houses in the Parish of Bodenham, Herefordshire

in the Township of Bodenham Devereux

by
Anthea Brian
with illustrations by
Averil Otiv

LOGASTON PRESS
Little Logaston, Logaston,
Woonton, Almeley, Herefordshire HR3 6QH

First published by Logaston Press 2004
Copyright © Anthea Brian 2004

ISBN 1 904396 14 3

Set in Garamond and Gill Sans by Logaston Press
and printed in Great Britain by
Bell & Bain Ltd., Glasgow

Acknowledgements

I have had a great deal of help in gathering the information presented here and am very grateful to the following: Miss Bucklee, Mr Bruce Copplestone-Crow, Mr S. Davies, Mr Duncan James, Mr K. Payton, Mrs Liz Philips and the staff of the Herefordshire Record Office and of the Hereford Cathedral Library for help with historical material and also to a number of people who live or have lived in Bodenham who have contributed their memories of earlier days, especially Mr Acton, Mr Trevor Barra, Mr Harley Dance, Mr Fred Downes, Mrs W. Jaine, Mr Derek Knott, Mr and Mrs Tom Rushton and Mr Jack Weyman-Jones.

In a work of this type some mistakes are probably inevitable. The author would be very glad to have these pointed out and would also be glad to hear of any more relevant information.

Finally, I am particularly indebted to the Woolhope Naturalists' Field Club who have given a very generous grant towards the costs of publication.

Any profits from the sale of this book will go towards further publications of historical information about Bodenham Parish.

The Township of Bodenham Devereux

a) The Five Townships

Bodenham is a very large parish but it has always been divided into several parts. At the time of Domesday the area fell into ten separate estates but by the nineteenth century the divisions, now called Townships, had been reduced to five, Bodenham Devereux, Bodenham Moor, Bowley, Maund Bryan and Whitchurch Maund. Broadfield was included in Bowley, the Vern in Bodenham Devereux and the Venn in Bodenham Moor. (The name Devereux derives from Evreux from whence the Devereux family came to England at the time of the Conquest, over the years the name has been anglicised and may be pronounced nowadays with the X sounding).

The name Bodenham Devereux seems never to have been in common usage but it is a convenient name for the part of the parish which is often referred to nowadays as 'the old village', a name that is not really correct since all parts of the parish are old. However the fact that the church is situated in Bodenham Devereux has had the effect of making that township the focal point of the parish. Furthermore the name for the whole parish, which is said to mean 'Boda's land in a river-bend', implies that the first settlement was also in this area since the part of the River Lugg that flows through Bodenham parish lies almost entirely in that township.

This study of the houses of the parish has begun with the township of Bodenham Devereux largely because it is the one for which most documentary evidence exists. This is because at some stage in the nineteenth century nearly every property in the township had been acquired by the Hampton Court estate under the Arkwrights. They not only kept meticulous records of their own transactions but on leaving the estate had the generosity to deposit all their own records, together with those they had inherited on buying the estate, in the Hereford Record Office.

b) Sources of information

Studying the history of this area had been like doing a three dimensional jigsaw that has some of its pieces missing and some broken. The third dimension is time while the 'pieces' are represented by the individual properties; 'missing pieces' are properties with no title deeds and 'broken pieces' those whose title deeds do not describe their bounds properly. The study has concentrated mainly on the eighteenth to twentieth centuries for which period the most information is inevitably available. The main sources consulted have been:

    a) National records such as the ten-yearly census.

    b) The Enclosure map and Apportionment of Bodenham, 1813. This has provided an invaluable framework despite the fact that its cover of the area was not complete. The

The Parish of Bodenham showing the Townships

surveyors were only concerned with land that at that time was still unenclosed and lying in open fields and so they left out all that was already enclosed. The Commissioners responsible for the enclosures apportioned the Tithes at the same time unfortunately and as a result Bodenham does not have a Tithe Map which would have given complete coverage and at a rather later date. (Venn and Vern have Tithe maps)

    c) <u>Parish Records</u> Bodenham is well provided with the usual type of parish record, vestry books, registers, poor law documents etc but is lucky to have an additional source of interesting material, the first parish magazines. These were written by the Rev Herbert Court Sturges, vicar from 1889 to 1900. (These have been made available through the kindness of two of his granddaughters, Mrs Tu and Mrs Penelope Eynor). Rev Sturges was a keen local historian who listened to what the older inhabitants of his time told him and wrote it down.

He was also a keen photographer. It is very probable that he would have written a parish history himself but sadly he died very suddenly, leaving only odd notes.

d) <u>Manorial Records</u> These go much further back in time and deal with pre-enclosure Bodenham.

e) <u>Estate Records</u> Three families have been important in the history of Bodenham Devereux;

(i) the Devereux family from whom came the first three Earls of Essex and whose records, when the title died out, passed to the Thynne family and are now therefore held mainly at Longleat.

(ii) the Conyngsby family of Hampton Court, some of whose records passed in the female line, confusingly, to a much later Earl of Essex and are held in the Hereford Record Office. (Where there might be confusion between the Earls of Essex the, surname, Devereux or Coningsby, is given in brackets after the title)

(iii) the Arkwright family of Hampton Court, all of whose Bodenham records were generously given to the newly formed Hereford Record Office. (HRO)

f) <u>Memories</u> The memories of a number of people who live or have lived in Bodenham for a long time have been invaluable.

c) The Names of Houses

Earlier on only the larger houses had individual, well established names and these rarely changed. Other houses and cottages were usually named after the person who lived there and as the occupant changed so did the name by which the house was known. More recently house names have changed more frequently and these changes make for difficulties when tracing the history of a house.

To try to clarify the matter when a house has had several names they are all given in the heading, the present name being given first.

d) Dating the Houses

Putting an exact date on an old house is probably impossible unless a dated reference to the actual building is found, something that is very rare, or unless a dendrochronological study has been carried out. Even finding the phrase 'newly erected' in a deed can be very misleading because the phrase may have been copied from one document to the next unchanged for years. Most dating is therefore only approximate and based on style but never the less, when this is done by an expert, it is probably fairly accurate. Several Bodenham houses were surveyed and photographed by the Royal Commission for Historic Monuments (RCHM) in the 1930s and where firm dates have been given in this booklet they have been taken from this work. Mr J.W.Tonkin has also kindly looked at some of Bodenham's buildings. If the deeds relating to a property have been found then the Hereford Record Office reference number is given after the name of the house.

e) The Illustrations

The drawings have been made from old photographs of varying quality and only buildings that have altered substantially or have disappeared altogether have been illustrated.

Index to Houses and other features in the Township of Bodenham Devereux

The names of buildings that are no longer standing are given in brackets

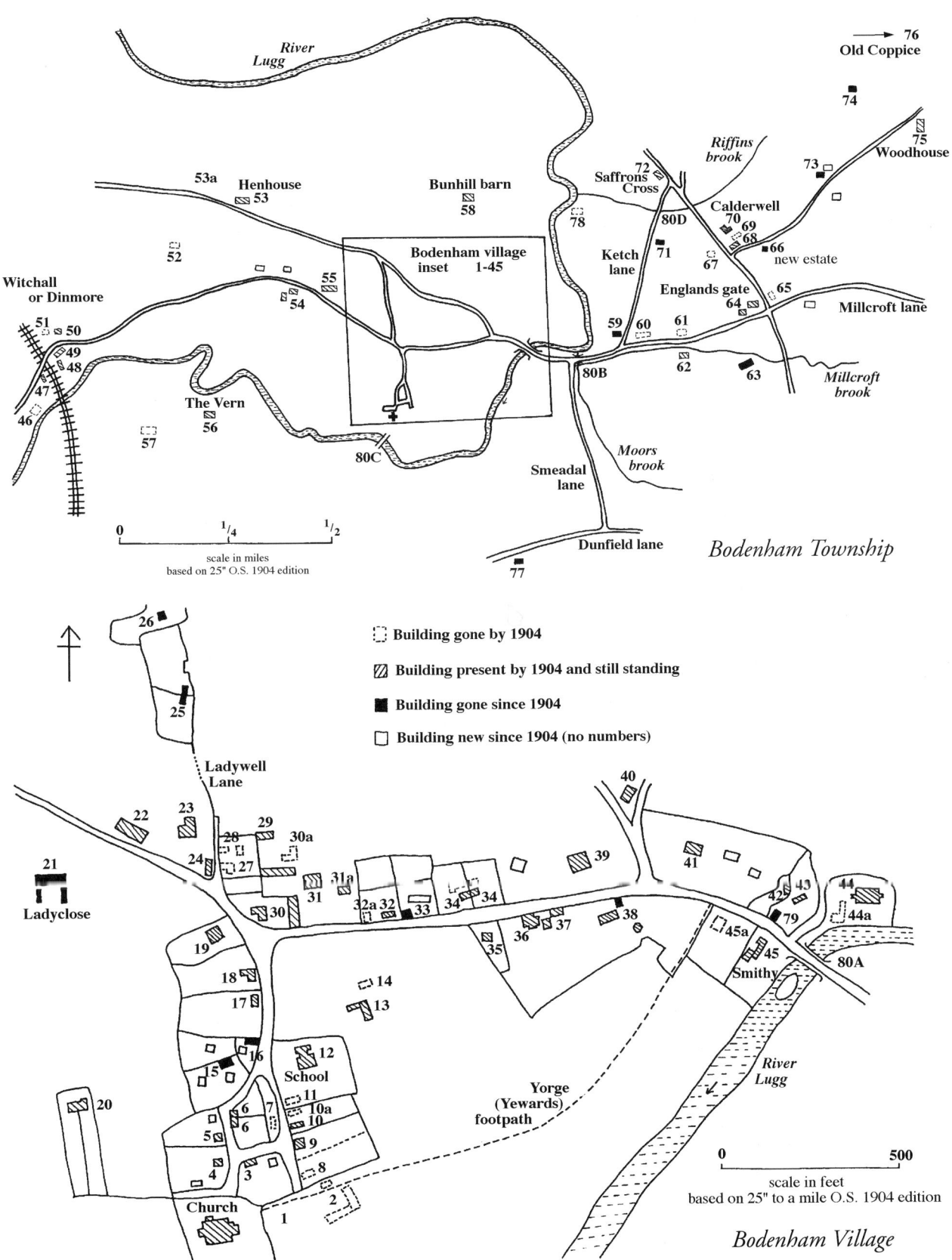

River Lugg

→ **76**
Old Coppice

74

75
Woodhouse

Riffins brook

53a Henhouse
53

Bunhill barn
58

72 Saffrons Cross

73

80D

Calderwell
70
69
68
66 new estate
67

52

Bodenham village inset 1-45

Ketch lane
71

Englands gate
64
65
Millcroft lane

55
54

Witchall or Dinmore

51 **50**
49
48
47
46

59 **60** **61**
62
63

80B

Millcroft brook

The Vern
56

57

80C

Moors brook

Smeadal lane

Dunfield lane

77

0   1/4   1/2

scale in miles
based on 25" O.S. 1904 edition

Bodenham Township

↑

26

25

Ladywell Lane

Building gone by 1904

Building present by 1904 and still standing

Building gone since 1904

Building new since 1904 (no numbers)

40

22 **23**

28 **29**

24 **27** **30a**

41

39

42 **43** **44**

21

Ladyclose

31a

31 **32a 32** **33** **34** **34**

79 **44a**

30

36 **37** **38**

45a

45
Smithy

80A

19

35

18

17

14

13

16
15 **12**
School

Yorge (Yewards) footpath

River Lugg

20

11
6 **7** **10a**
5 **6** **10**

9

4 **3** **8**

Church

1

2

0   500

scale in feet
based on 25" to a mile O.S. 1904 edition

Bodenham Village

5

(1) The First Parsonage House and its site / Bodenham Regis Manor (A63 / 11 / 192)

Bodenham has always had an absentee Rector and over the years his deputy, the Vicar, has lived in at least four different houses in the village often well away from the church. But the earlier priests, one of whom was recorded in Domesday Book, probably lived in a house on a site just east of the church, a site which today is occupied by the churchyard extension made in 1982.

The Norman family who held the Manor of Bodenham before and after the Conquest founded Brecon Priory *c.*1105 and endowed their new foundation with the church of Bodenham and all its lands and revenues. As a result from that time onwards until the Dissolution of the monasteries in 1537 the Vicars of Bodenham were appointed by the priors of Brecon. The names of fifteen of these vicars are known and Richard Morris was the last of them. His dwelling was probably still on the old parsonage site east of the church

At the Dissolution the lands of Brecon Priory were taken over by the Crown and so it was Henry VIII who appointed the next Vicar, one William Lloyd. He was followed by James Yeoman who was appointed by Queen Mary in 1556. Then in 1557 Queen Mary and her husband Philip granted the 'manor of Bodenham Regis' to Sir Humphrey Conningsby of Hampton Court in an impressive document with a large red seal. In this the land granted was described as; 'all that manor of Bodenham with the advowson situate next to the cemetery of Bodenham with one garden, a columbarium and two closes of land adjacent which formerly were once devised to Richard Morris, clerk'. The name Bodenham Regis persisted for quite a time.

In 1699 Sir Humphrey's descendant, Lord Coningsby, leased the site to his tenant at Devereux Court and by then it was described as 'the capital messuage now much ruined and decayed known as the Parsonage farm and two barns known as the Tithe barns'.

Elsewhere the 'Parsonage House' was described as adjoining the churchyard on the east side and as late as 1813 this field was still being called 'parsonage meadow'. Part of it was incorporated in the new churchyard extension and here stones in lines have been found when fresh graves are dug which may have formed the stone foundations of a timber-framed house. It seems that after 1699 this house was neither repaired nor replaced and must finally have disappeared. Since it was described as a capital messuage it must have been of high status and a few timbers from just such a medieval house have been found built into other, later, houses in the village.

Sadly the columbarium had disappeared by 1699 but the two closes of land near the house were probably the two fields known as Upper and Lower Yorge. Earlier spellings of this name indicate that it was really 'yard' a name that was formerly used for a large enclosure near a dwelling. The name has survived today in the name of the public footpath that crosses these fields. Within living memory this path was called 'yewards' and the Bodenham W.I. recorded a tradition that it could never be closed because a queen had once walked on it. It is tempting to wonder if this tradition goes back to the time when Queen Mary owned this part of the village in the sixteenth century and for a time it was called Bodenham Regis. Certainly no royal connection with any other part of the parish has been found and it seems an odd coincidence that the tradition reported by the W.I. and Bodenham's only royal charter should both refer to the same part of the village.

(2) The Two Tithe Barns

The two Tithe Barns were mentioned in the lease of 1699 described under the First Parsonage Site (1). They were presumably built to house the tithes of grain collected for the Rector . There is no doubt where these barns stood because they are marked on the 1813 Enclosure Map, two large buildings, each almost as long as the church, standing at right angles to each other in the field to the east of the church. They can actually be seen in a landscape painted by John Varley from the top of the hill to the north at some time before 1813 where he too shows two large buildings standing at right angles to each other just to the east of the church.

In 1813 the field in which the barns stood was called 'parsonage meadow' and at that time it belonged to the Vicar. In 1846 a new vicar was installed at Bodenham. He was the Rev. Henry Arkwright, nephew of John Arkwright, the owner of the Hampton Court estate at that time. A new vicarage was built for him (see 55) and in preparation for this there had to be an exchange of land between the estate and the glebe. It seems that under the previous vicar the Hampton Court estate had managed the glebe lands as well as the estate and there was considerable confusion as to just which lands were part of the glebe. To sort this out the agent for the estate interviewed the three oldest men in the village and they all agreed that the two barns, that had stood beside the church, had been moved. One was moved to Bodenham Court Farm and the other, almost certainly, was moved rather further and is now known as the Bunhill Barn. Both these barns have numerous empty peg holes and mortice joints and show other signs of having been taken apart and put together again. Their later histories are described under the relevant numbers (31 & 58).

(3) Peasegreen Cottage

This cottage is said to have been built in the seventeenth century and one of the earlier inhabitants was probably Thomas Sandford, a shoemaker who with his wife was described at the time as a papist. The Sandford family seem to have owned the cottage for many years. One of them married a William Davies and their family owned the house up to the twentieth century.

Unlike most other Bodenham properties this one did not come into the ownership of the Arkwrights and when at last it was offered to them the agent 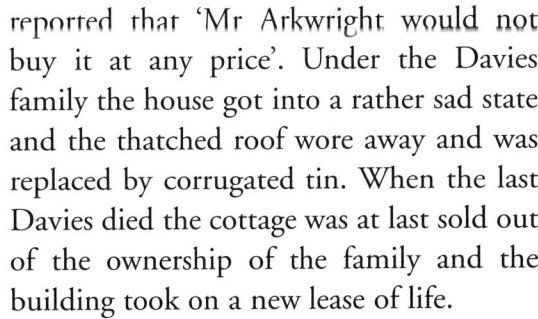 reported that 'Mr Arkwright would not buy it at any price'. Under the Davies family the house got into a rather sad state and the thatched roof wore away and was replaced by corrugated tin. When the last Davies died the cottage was at last sold out of the ownership of the family and the building took on a new lease of life.

Peasegreen Cottage

(4) Church House (A63 / 11 / 235)

This house was built in the seventeenth century but its title deeds begin in the early eighteenth century when it was owned by Richard Powles, a butcher. He was followed by John and then Elizabeth Goode and then in 1836 by William and Elizabeth Jenkins. In the same year they gave up the house to Richard Arkwright of Hampton Court in exchange for the White House (18) and William Mytton, an agricultural labourer moved in. The estate gave the house a thorough overhaul which included a new roof of stone tiles, probably from the estate quarry on Dinmore Hill. After this four generations of the Mytton family occupied the house for about 150 years buying it from the estate in 1923.

Church House

(5) Belle Ville / Newton's Cottage, Pease Green (B76/Box 13)

The earlier small cottage on this site was demolished and rebuilt on the same spot quite recently with a considerably raised roof. The timber-frame structure revealed during demolition was of thin, flimsy timbers built against a large, stone chimney stack at the rear. This type of structure fits well with the earliest description for this site found in the title deeds of 1791 which states; 'it is supposed that the cottage was built on the waste'.

This indicates that Pease Green was formerly an open space—a real village green—and Belle Ville started life as a squatters cottage built on this piece of manorial waste (see section 83).

In 1791 Michael Newton, the second son of James Newton, tenant of Devereux Court (20) inherited the property from Abraham Bowker of Calderwell (68) and Michael's son, who had moved away from Bodenham, sold it in 1842 to the Hampton Court estate. Under the estate the cottage went under the name of 'Newton's cottage' as was the custom then. The name 'Belle Ville' only replaced it quite recently and is supposed to have been taken from the name of an Irish race horse.

(6) Churchwalk Cottages, Peasegreen (A63/ 11 / 169 , AL5/7 & B76 / Box 5)

These two semi-detached cottages are made of different materials and were built at different times. The southern cottage, which is timber-framed, was built in the seventeenth century and the stone cottage to the north in the 1820s. Before 1664 the timber-framed cottage was owned by a Thomas Taylor of Canon Frome and said to be 'near a place called Pease Green'. It had with it seven acres of arable land dispersed in the common fields of Bodenham and two and a half acres of meadow held in four separate parcels. Clearly it was a small subsistence farm.

In 1705 the cottage was sold to Lord Coningsby of Hampton Court and as a result came into the possession of Richard Arkwright when he bought the estate in the early nineteenth century.

Then in 1820 Richard Arkwright gave the cottage to Richard Yeoman, a stone mason, in exchange for a cottage up Ladywell Lane (26). Richard Yeoman built a new stone cottage onto the existing timber-framed one and then in 1820 sold both cottages back to the Hampton Court estate. At that time there was a pigscot, a shed and a privy hidden by laurel bushes in the garden. These were probably present in all the cottage gardens but are not often mentioned.

Under the estate both cottages had a succession of tenants and when the estate was divided up and sold in 1923 they were bought by Mr James Simpson who was the church organist and lived at the Weirhouse(44). Soon after James Simpson sold off the eastern end of the cottage gardens to Dinmore Estates Ltd (see under 7) and then in 1935 sold both cottages to a builder.

(7) Car park site / Howarth's Cottage. Peasegreen (A63 / I I / 229)

This small area once held a house and the title deeds begin in 1723 when John Howarth who lived there sold the house, garden and 'backside' to a James Jones of Leominster. He kept it for 20 years during which time the house, which was probably of flimsy timber-frame construction, fell or was taken down, though its barn remained. In 1742 the site was bought by the Rev George Coningsby DD, Vicar of Bodenham and a relative of the Hampton Court family. He left Bodenham to become Rector of Pencombe in 1756 and a year later sold the site to William Hall of Pencombe. At that time it was described as: 'a parcel of ground now used as a garden ... and has for many years been used by John Monk, on part whereof was formerly a messuage where John Howarth did dwell'.

William Hall then bought Pump Cottage (32) and moved down to Bodenham. He, his son and grandson, all called William Hall, continued to own the site which in 1800 was described as: 'an orchard known by the name of Pease Green with barn and cider mill'.

Then in 1819 the third William Hall sold it to Thomas Tarbutt of Riffins Mill (Bowley) who ten years later sold it to Richard Arkwright. From then on for a hundred years as part of the Hampton Court estate it became the gardens for Churchwalk Cottages (6) and so, when these were sold to James Simpson, this area went with them.

Then in 1931 James Simpson sold the site to Dinmore Manor estate and it opened a quarry for gravel there, right in the middle of the village. Worse was to follow for when the quarrying ended the hole left behind became a rat-infested rubbish dump. The large pile of scrap metal collected during World War Two, for which Bodenham was commended in the local newspaper, may have been accumulated here.

It was only in the 1970s that the dump was closed and the area surfaced after which what had been John Howarth's house and garden became the car park we have today.

(8) Cottage that once stood south of the Old Post Office (B76 / 5)

The earliest evidence about this cottage comes in 1734 when it was used as security for a mortgage on another property in the village. A subsequent deed of 1760 gives the information that in 1734 one William Monk had been granted a lease by Margaret, Countess Conyngsby for 99 years of the ground on which the cottage stood. It sounds very much as though the cottage had been put up around 1734 on the manorial waste of Pease Green and that this lease legalised the act. If so, like

Belle Ville (5), the structure was probably rather flimsy which might account for its non-survival. One of the tenants of the cottage was a Mr Bethel who, in the days before there was a clock in the church tower, rang one of the church bells every day at 6am and 8pm.

In 1836 a descendant of William Monk, Ann wife of Hugh Gladding, exchanged the cottage with Richard Arkwright for the cottage now called The Retreat (35). The estate then put new stone tiles on the roof and erected the stone slab fence beside the road that still stands today.

One of the tenants of the refurbished cottage was Joseph Daniel who was described as a cordwainer, shopkeeper and butcher. He was followed by James Colebourne junior whose father was tenant of Bodenham Court Farm (31). Although this was the main farm in the village and his father was an important man the younger James Colebourne seems to have been an aimless individual who had various jobs and sometimes none. His was the last family to occupy this cottage and when he left it was 'pulled down' in April 1877. The land was added to the garden of the Old Post Office (9) next door.

One of James Colebourne's children emigrated to New Zealand but never forgot Bodenham and wrote regularly to the Vicar and the school sending them a copy of the *Illustrated Aukland News*. In 1931 the letters stopped coming and they found out that he had been killed in an earthquake.

(9) The Old Post Office

This cottage was built in the seventeenth century and was probably one of a group of properties bought by Lord Coningsby of Hampton Court about 1705. If so it had formerly been owned by a Mr Robert Green and his tenant had been William Jones, the parish clerk.

As part of the Hampton Court estate the cottage would have been sold to Richard Arkwright in 1810 but it is not specifically mentioned, because it formed a part of Bodenham Court Farm (31). From the time of William Jones onwards this cottage seems always to have housed the parish clerk and since he of course was literate at a time when many people could not read and write it is not surprising that one of the clerks at least ran a school here. This was Richard Reynolds who was clearly a very energetic man and who has left many records of his activities including a pew list for the church. (He worked this out twice, allowing two different lengths of pew per person). One of his school pupils was Mary Wright who lived at Bank House (41) and whose parents paid six pence a week for her schooling. Mary's father, Thomas Wright, subsequently became the parish clerk himself and moved down to the Old Post Office. Mary Wright married a

Old Post Office

John Harford who had come to the parish as Surveyor and Collector of the Parish Rates. He was employed by Bodenham Vestry and when Thomas Wright died succeeded him as Parish Clerk. Then around 1860 he took on the Post Office as well which had formerly been at Englands Gate (64).

John Harford died in 1882 and Mary moved away from the village but she was buried at Bodenham and the Vicar described her as; 'one of the links that bind us to the past , it is very rare nowadays for a person living to 84 to have been baptised, married and buried in the same parish'. The house remained as the Post Office after the Harfords' time and the new post master was William Henry Smalley. When he died the PO remained in the hands of Mrs Smalley and her daughter Rosa who later married Mr Pound of the Whitehouse (18).The P.O. was then moved to Pound Cottage (42). Note the letter box and the handles of the mail cart in the shed on the right.

(10 & 10a) Peasegreen (A63 / 11 / 234 & B 76/7)

The title deeds of the property start in 1743 with the will of Daniel Wright, a 'blacksmith of the Penthouse' (39) who left it to his son John Wright, one Thomas Baker being the tenant. In 1770 John and his son Thomas were fined at the manorial court for 'not turning out an encroachment on the Lady's waste in the village of Bodenham'. The Lady of the manor was Lady Coningsby and it is possible that the part of the waste involved lay to the north of the cottage where the Wrights had built another cottage, a very small one (10a). When Thomas Wright made his will in 1813 he left this other cottage to his grandson George Wright on condition that George's mother, Elizabeth daughter of Thomas, should have it for her lifetime.

Peasegreen

Thomas Wright left the main cottage to his son Daniel who in 1834 sold it to the Arkwrights. Under the Hampton Court estate a pig sty was built and the cottage was regularly thatched and white-washed. At one time, although probably only two rooms up and two down, it housed a family of five children with three lodgers in addition. Later, probably after the death of Elizabeth, the tiny cottage(10a) was pulled down and its land was added to the garden of the main cottage.

(11) Cottage that stood on the school site

This seems to have been another of Bodenham's short-lived cottages. It was not marked on the Enclosure map of 1812 but was shown on a map of around 1840 when it was clearly marked just south of the Vicarage in the field (13). It seems possible that this cottage was built by the vicar, the Rev Waite Robinson, to house someone working for him and a hint of this is given in a note by

Benjamin Wanklin, head carpenter for the Hampton Court estate when he wrote, 'I had the management of everything for Mr Robinson in pulling down and putting up buildings'. It is not known when the cottage was taken down.

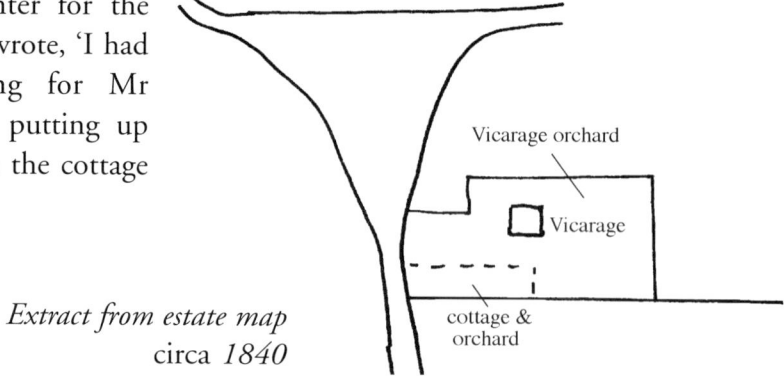

Extract from estate map circa 1840

(12) The School and earlier schools in the parish
The present school
The site of the school was given to the vicar and churchwardens by John Hungerford Arkwright of Hampton Court in 1862 when it was described as: 'a parcel of an orchard called Vicarage orchard'. Mr Arkwright gave both the site and the money to build the school (and also a school at Maund Common) The school was finished in 1864 and Mr Morton, who at that time was in charge of a school at the Weirhouse (44), moved his pupils up to the new building.

Since then there have been various additions to the building and the school bell was removed to Leominster museum. A carved stone shield was removed from over a window at the same time but this was saved from destruction by Mrs Jayne and now (1980s) lies in the field below Devereux Court.

Earlier schools
The benefactions board in the ringing chamber in the church tower records that Nicholas Mason of Howton, who died in 1811, left £30 to be paid out of Bitterley Hyde (in Pencombe) to establish and support a school in Bodenham. This school was set up and Richard Reynolds, the parish clerk, was the schoolmaster. His school was held in an ordinary house said to have been first in the Isle of Rhea and then at Pease Green (9). But there is evidence in 1818 of a school also being held at Tan-y-Bryn (17).

Richard Reynolds died in 1822 and the next school may have been kept, according to the parish magazine in the 1930s, by 'Thomas Daw's father opposite the Millcroft (62) where formerly three houses stood'.

By 1832 a school was being held in a part of Devereux Court (20) and later this was moved to the Weir House (44). Both these buildings were provided by the Arkwright family who from now on seem to have taken on responsibility for the education of the children of Bodenham, generosity that culminated in their gift of the present school building and its site.

This was very fortunate for the people of Bodenham for by now the descendants of Nicholas Mason, the original benefactor, were refusing to go on paying the money out of Bitterley Hyde. The vicar and church wardens went to court about this in 1857 but to no avail.

(13) 'The Barn' / farm buildings / former Vicarage and other buildings that stood nearby

The large field east of the village green and south of the main road through the village was formerly known as 'Vicarage Orchard' and the stone building standing in this field next door to the school was Bodenham's Vicarage in the eighteenth century and officially so up to 1844 when a new Vicarage (55) was built. The last vicar to actually live in this house was Rev. Nicholas Waite Robinson who came to the parish in 1799 but although he remained vicar until 1842 when he died, he had by that time been living for many years in Cheltenham on grounds of ill health. His curate meanwhile had lived at Bodenham Hall (23) and during this period the vicarage began to fall into disrepair. From then on it was used as a barn and cow-shed for Bodenham Court Farm (31) right up to the 1990s when it was sold and made into a house again.

It is clear from old deeds that a number of other buildings once stood in Vicarage Orchard and irregularities in the ground surface and the finding of stone foundations when laying pipes confirms this. Reg Jones, who lived and worked in the village for many years, told of finding a pitched stone path, like that leading today to the church lych gate, but in this case the path was leading to the former Vicarage. Perhaps these are two ends of the same path which led from the church to the Vicarage.

Although no documentary evidence has been found it is probable that an earlier house on this site became the vicarage around 1542 when the vicar ceased to live at the Old Parsonage site (1). Up to 1547 Bodenham had three chantries and each had a house where the chantry priest lived. When the chantries were suppressed Bodenham's vicar might have been housed in one of these vacant houses, perhaps one that stood on this site.

Rather little except for their names is known of Bodenham's early vicars until 1647 when John Pember was installed. His vicarage fairly certainly stood on this site. He was deposed in 1647 but returned with the Restoration of the monarchy at which time the churchwardens reported that 'Our vicarage house and outhouse is in good repair'. John Pember was a man of substance and a Prebendary of Hereford cathedral. A tablet in the church records his death in 1677 and his will has been preserved also the inventory that listed his possessions room by room so giving a description of his vicarage:

> In the parlour - 1 table, 1 form, 1 side cupboard, bed, bedstead, andirons, a clock
> In the hall - a table, 1 form, chairs, 3 spits, links, pothooks, fowling gun
> In the chambers - 3 beds, boulsters, coverings, chairs & other furniture
> In the syder house - hogsheads,   In the Flax house - a malt mill,
> Grain, hay, bees, money over £70, debts £5, wearing apparel £10, a study of books £30

While living in the vicarage John Pember bought a property next door, just to the north, and he may well have lived here through the Commonwealth times. On his death his four sons sold this property to the next vicar, Rev. William Caldecott. His widow sold it to a Robert Green who in 1705 sold it to Lord Coningsby of Hampton Court. The deeds to this property survive and are described as 'old writings belonging to tenement near the vicarage of Bodenham'. After this successive vicars rented this property from Hampton Court the last being the Rev Lucas Hathway who occupied it 'sans lease' and for no rent. Was this because he was Lord Coningsby's son-in-law or was it because the building had fallen down? About this time there is documentary evidence of other houses in this area as well.

Former Vicarage

The next vicar was Rev George Coningsby, also a member of the Hampton Court family and a person of importance. This makes it likely that the stone building that we have today was built by or for him. Since Lord Coningsby at this time owned all the land to the north of the Vicarage he may have swept away all the houses in this area to make a suitable estate around the Vicarage, leaving only one cottage to house a servant (14).

Two ornamental trees that may well have been planted in the Vicarage garden at this time survived to the 1950s. One was a huge Tulip tree that was taken down when new buildings were added to the school and the other was the 'second largest Box tree in the county', a stump of which still stood just north of the school till the 1970s.

(14) Cottage in Vicarage Orchard (taken down 1870)

This was a building that has left very little evidence of its presence but just enough to be sure that it actually existed. It is marked on the 1813 map just north of the Vicarage (13) and in an entry under Bodenham Court Farm the estate agent in his Buildings Record notes 'new oven at labourers cottage near Rectory £1-5-1'. The next mention comes in the agent's Day Book in 1854 when he notes: 'Elizabeth Barber dies who lived in cottage in Bodenham and Colebourne applies for it for widow and four children, name of Burlton'.

Colebourn was the tenant at Bodenham Court Farm (31) and he got his way for in 1860 the agent recorded 'Cottage late Barber let to Mr Colebourne for Mrs Burton'. The census records the family: Esther Burton, widow aged 45, William, aged 16, carter boy and three 'scholars'; Sarah, 14, Emma, 12 and Thomas, 9.

Nine years later comes the last entry about this cottage, 'Taking down old cottage (late Burton) 10s'. There obviously was not much to take down and there is no mention of using the stone or timber elsewhere as was often the case.

(15) Rose Cottage and (16) Fred Williams' Cottage (both gone)

These two cottages occupied an important place visually in the Pease Green area of the village until they were both demolished sometime in the late 1960s.

Rose Cottage was the older and the only one of the two to be shown on the 1813 Enclosure map. Although its timber-frame structure was clearly visible from the outside it was not listed in the RCHM survey and this means that the surveyor considered that it was built after 1715. The thinness of the timbers visible in the photograph would bear this out. It was two storeys high and had an outbuilt chimney at the west end. Possibly the whole west wall was stone with a wooden lean-to shed against it.

Fred Williams' Cottage was built some time between 1813 and 1887, probably on land that had gone with Rose Cottage. It was made of stone with a tiled roof and had a brick privy which was retained to be used as a garden shed. Some of the stones from the house were very large and one, about 8 feet by 2 feet, was too large to be removed and was made into the base of a rockery.

Rose Cottage

Neither of these two cottages formed part of the Hampton Court estate and so there is rather little early information about them. In 1806 John Lawrence was the probable owner of Rose Cottage when he was rated as owning a cottage with 3 roods, 9 perches of land which had been left to him by his father, also a John Lawrence, in 1793 when it was described as 'messuage at Pease Green'. Tenants around this time were John Griffiths, followed by William Crewson and Edward Bowcott, agricultural labourers.

By 1905 John Went of the Smithy (45) was the owner and he sold both cottages to William Pritchard Williams of Brockington Farm (63). After the latter died his two sons in 1918 sold all their Bodenham properties and shortly after these two cottages were bought by the Medlicotts of Bodenham Court Farm (31). Fred Williams was their carter and lived in the stone cottage (16).

Later the cottages were sold with Bodenham Court Farm to Lady Hereford and it was said to be the young Lord Hereford who had both cottages pulled down, Rose Cottage on a Good Friday and Fred Williams Cottage after it was first burnt out, leaving just a heap of stone. This was done to make a drive to the Moat House (20) where the Dowager Lady Hereford intended to live, a plan that never came off.

Later Mr and Mrs Jaine acquired the site and built three bungalows there. According to Mrs Jayne no title deeds could be produced but Lady Hereford helped the Jaines to establish their title, in gratitude for which they called the larger bungalow Ladymead. The absence of Title deeds together with the late, rather flimsy building of these two cottages indicates that they too may have been built on the 'manorial waste' of Pease Green.

(17) Tan - y - Bryn / Ivy Cottage / Lower House Cottage

No old title deeds to this house have been found and there is some doubt about when it was built because most of the timbers had earlier been used in another building to judge by the number of empty mortices and peg holes. In particular this applies to one large tie beam which must have been made for a much older house with a quite different type of structure.

The earliest documentary evidence found comes from the Rate Lists of 1806–1823. These all show that the cottage was owned by one Nicholas Sirell. In 1814 it was described as 'new tenement and garden' and then in 1818 as 'school, cottage and garden'. These rate lists were almost certainly accurate because they were copied out by Richard Reynolds, the very active parish clerk who was also the schoolmaster. So it seems probable that around 1814 a new cottage was built using some old timbers from older, disused buildings and that for a short time Richard Reynolds held his school here (see 9).

Nicholas Sirrell also owned the Pigeon House (38). He left both properties to his daughter Mary Wynne and in 1850 she sold them both to the Hampton Court estate. At that time this cottage was called Lower House cottage and was occupied by Thomas Gatehouse, junior (see 25) who was a gardener at Hampton Court.

Then in 1912 Mr Bailey bought the cottage from the estate together with the Pigeon House and his gardener, Morgan, lived here. The Pigeon House was sold after Mr Bailey and his second wife had died but the family held on to the cottage until the last of the Morgan family died when it was sold in 1967 to Mr and Mrs Passey. They found the place in a very bad state with ivy all over, inside as well as out, hence its new name, Ivy Cottage.

Unfortunately somewhere along the line of owners the old title deeds have got lost. They would have been included in the Pigeon House deeds but when that house was sold in the 1980s no old deeds came to light.

(18) The White House / Roger's tenement (AL5 / 10)

As far as documentation is concerned the history of this house falls into three periods:

a) The early years up to 1810 when Richard Arkwright bought it.

b) 1810 to 1836 when, as part of the Hampton Court estate, the agent's records give good information.

c) 1836 onwards, after the estate had exchanged this house with Church House (4) (without handing over any title deeds to the new owner).

(a) In 1699 Coningsby Pembruge, the tenant of Devereux Court (20) bought three messuages from a John Winton. Two of these have been identified as Well Cottage (30) and Lower Lady Well Lane cottage (25). The third was described as: 'a messuage at a place called the cross', a description that fits this house well.

Almost at once the three properties were mortgaged to a Richard Rogers and then in 1705 were sold to Lord Coningsby of Hampton Court. On the outside of the bundle of deeds is written: 'writings for lands purchased of Pembruge that was mortgaged to Rogers'. It seems that since the White House, in common with most other houses in Bodenham, had no name, the name of 'Rogers' stuck to it. Over the next hundred years some information about the property comes from the Land Tax records and these show that 'Rogers tenement' was first occupied with the Parsonage Farm (1) by Grace Wright and then by a Joseph South, possibly as his retirement home. (see 34 and 44).

(b) After Richard Arkwright bought the Hampton Court estate, including Rogers tenement, more information becomes available. In 1820 Miss Elizabeth Newman was the tenant and although no longer called Rogers tenement we know that her house was certainly the house known formerly as Rogers tenement because of an argument between Miss Newman and the agent. The agent intended to put the rent up for the new tenant but Miss Newman said that she expected to pay the same rent as Joseph South who had been tenant before her. One suspects that she got her way for after that she was always in arrears with her rent and sometimes was given notice to quit—though the threat was never carried out. She was clearly a woman who considered herself of some importance; always called Miss Newman and being allowed to arrange repairs to the house herself, with materials provided by the estate.

(c) The last we hear of Miss Newman (or possibly her niece, another Miss Newman) is in 1837 when the agent recorded that she: 'ceased to pay rent on this cottage being exchanged with Mrs Goode for a cottage with land'. From this date the owner's title deeds take up the story. At first the house was owned by William and Elizabeth Jenkins, Elizabeth probably being Mrs Goode's daughter. At this time Miss Newman went on as the tenant but by 1851 the Jenkins family were living there, William being a gardener. On his death his son let the house to James Morton, the head teacher at the school. Then after many changes of owner it was bought by Frederick Charles Pound who later married Rosa Smalley of the Old Post Office (9). The large holly tree in the garden has the initials of Mr Pound's son carved in the bark which, due to the elasticity of holly bark, are still present, though considerably enlarged by the growth of the trunk.

(19) The Hollies / Well Cottage / Well Villa / The Villa / The Cross Farm

The history of this house, its occupiers and owners is very tied up with that of Bodenham Hall (23). The oldest and probably the original name for the house was the Cross Farm, so called presumably because it stood beside the market cross on the village green.

In the early seventeenth century this property, like Bodenham Hall, formed a part of the estate of Hugh Walshe. From him it passed to the Clark family, father and son and then the Hollies on its own was sold to the Hill family, Richard Hill who died in 1684 and Thomas his son and heir. This Thomas was referred to as 'Thomas Hill of the Cross' in the manorial records to distinguish him from another of the same name living at Bodenham Hall. In 1690 he was ordered to repair the village stocks which presumably stood on the green. He died in 1712 and the inventory with his will says that he had: '8 horned beasts, 2 mares, 2 swine and corn in the barn etc'. His widow, Margaret, had to give up one red cow as a herriot.

Around 1740 John Reece bought both the Cross Farm and Bodenham Hall. He lived in the latter with his wife and niece, Mary Unett, but his farming operations were carried out from the Cross Farm, occupied by Benjamin Trumper On his death Mary Unett inherited both properties but one was already mortgaged and she was in constant financial trouble until she sold Bodenham Hall and moved across the road to live at the Cross Farm.

Clearly it did not come up to her standards and she set about altering it. The house was said to have been 'lately rebuilt upon or near a decayed messuage called the Cross Farm with barn' but, to judge by the timbers in the roof in the present house, this meant altering the existing house and not rebuilding it. Though now living in a smaller house Miss Unett clearly intended to maintain her status and insisted on continuing to sit in the Bodenham Hall pew in church, a tricky problem that the Hampton Court agent was called on to deal with. However Mary Unett was still living beyond her means and to pay for the work on the house she took out more mortgages. In the end in 1833 she was forced to sell this house too to the Arkwrights just a few months before she died.

The estate immediately sold the house to a Mr Wilkins, but without most of the farm land which was added to the lands of Bodenham Court Farm (31). This was the estate's policy at the time, to put all the land with one large farm and make what had formerly been farm houses into either cottages for the estate workmen or, if rather larger, to make them into gentlemen's residences.

George Wilkins probably bought the house because his wife Rhoda had a sister, Elizabeth Turberville, living over the road at Bodenham Hall. The little wicket gate still present in the wall by the road may well have been made at this time to allow quick comings and goings between the two houses. After George's death his widow left the Hollies to her niece, Rhoda Turberville, who had married the curate, Rev David Lewes. On the death of her husband Rhoda, with her daughter Emma Georgeanna, moved across the road from Bodenham Hall to the Hollies and they seem to have changed the name of the house from the Cross Farm to The Villa.

The next owner changed the name again to Well Cottage and the next, William Mosely, changed it yet again to the Hollies, a name that seems to have stuck. Mosely was followed by John and Mary Jane Baggot, brother and sister. Mary Jane had kept the shop (33) and continued to sell sweets to the children from a back window of the Hollies.

Around 1850 Bodenham's first resident doctor, John Woodyatt, occupied the Hollies for a short time. He was living there when the first Dinmore tunnel was completed and he and his wife went to a celebration dinner at the Green Dragon, Mrs Woodyatt in a crinoline with a red rose in her hair.

Dr John Woodyatt

A more recent owner was Mr Jack Weyman Jones who moved here from Bodenham Court Farm (31) when he retired from farming. His memories have contributed many details to this brief history of the village.

(20) Devereux Court / The Moat House / Bodenham Court / The Court

This was the site of the manor house for the demesne farm of the Manor of Bodenham Devereux. Its ownership was in the hands of the Devereux family and their descendants from the twelfth century until 1803. The manorial courts were held here and so it was variously known as Bodenham Court, Devereux Court or just 'the Court.'

In the fourteenth century Sir William Devereux and his son Sir Walter may have been resident in Bodenham. Sir Walter was granted a licence for a Tuesday market in Bodenham in 1379 and it seems probable that he or his father rebuilt Bodenham's earlier church and gave us the large, impressive nave of the church more or less as it still stands adjacent to their manor house. The lovely stone effigy of a lady with her small child lying in the chancel dates from this period and probably represents a Devereux wife. Later generations seem to have lost interest in the place and by the time a later Walter Devereux had been created first Earl of Essex in 1572 there was probably only a steward living in the house.

Robert Devereux, second Earl of Essex, was Queen Elizabeth's favourite and as a result national history impinged on Bodenham in a very tangible way. The lease of Devereux Court and its farm to Sir Thomas Coningsby in 1600 had to be confirmed by his countess the following year, 'following the death of her husband', a tactful way of describing his execution. Their son, another Robert, became the third Earl but died leaving no children and the title became extinct. The manor passed to Robert's sister the Duchess of Somerset who gave it to her grandson-in-law, Thomas Thynne, whose nephew became the first Marquis of Bath of Longleat. In this way the Bodenham property became a small appendage of a vast estate administered from far away in Wiltshire and was always leased out. The Thynne family did nothing for the village. They gave it no school or almshouses and left no mark on the church but they undoubtedly collected their rents regularly.

In 1670 a Mr Mayo was tenant of the Court and he was leasing 'the manor house and garden, fold and barn with one rickyard and the old orchard about 2 acres'. With this went about 86 acres of arable scattered among the open fields of the parish. There was said to be a shortage of orchard and no wood at all for firewood or for repairs. A final note stated that the estate 'is apt to be ffluded': one thing that has not changed.

In 1685 the manor was leased to Lord Coningsby of Hampton Court who sub-let the property to Coningsby Pembruge. In the lease it was described as 'capital messuage on site of the manor of Bodenham Devereux' and with it were leased the Parsonage Farm (1) and the two Tithe Barns (2). In 1708 the same group of properties were leased to John Mason the younger of Howton with Rogers tenement (39) and the Henhouse (52) as well and then in 1722 they were all let to William Newton.

By 1753 the Coningsby lease from Longleat had run out and after that William Newton leased the properties directly from the Marquis of Bath. He died in 1751 and his son James took on the tenancy. James died in 1802 and left his extensive possessions associated with the farm and valued at nearly £1,000 to his second son, Michael. The eldest son, James, was literally cut off with a shilling. Michael held the next annual court dinner at Devereux Court that year, as his father had done regularly in previous years, but by 1803 he had left the farm and moved to a small cottage (5).

1803 was the year that Devereux Court was sold for the first time in its history when the Marquis of Bath conveyed it, with all his Bodenham properties, to the Earl of Essex of Hampton Court. (This Earl of Essex was a Coningsby rather than a Devereux).

The first tenant under the new regime was Thomas West. Unfortunately detailed records of the seven years of the Earl of Essex's ownership have not been found but clearly they were years of great change. In particular the centre of the ancient manorial farm was shifted from Devereux Court (20) up to Bodenham Court Farm known earlier as Corbetts Farm (31) but in the absence of records of the work involved it is sometimes hard to distinguish between the two properties. The most likely sequence of events would seem to be that Devereux Court had become very badly run down during James Newton's latter years. He was 97 when he died and neither of his sons seem to have been competent farmers. During this period the Earl of Essex enlarged and modernised Corbetts farm (31) which he already owned and then, when he had bought Devereux Court, he ran the two farms together under Thomas West who lived at Corbetts Farm rather than Devereux Court. The remains of the Parsonage farm were also included in the property. The whole came to be known as Bodenham Court Farm and the name Corbetts Farm was dropped. The actual house of Devereux Court was allowed to fall more and more into disrepair and it was let to the overseers of the poor.

This was the situation Richard Arkwright found when he bought the Hampton Court estate. Devereux Court, the oldest house in the village, was not even mentioned in the sale catalogue and in 1823 was described as being in 'a very ruinous state of repair'. Never-the-less Richard Arkwright had it repaired and made into four cottages two of which were later made into a school. When the school moved out it became a 'double cottage' and was always know as the Moat House. It went on like this after the sale of the whole estate in 1923 owned first by Mr Medlicot of Bodenham Court Farm (31), then by Lady Hereford who had some idea of making it into a dower house, an idea that came to nothing (see 15). Later it was made into one dwelling again and the name changed again from the Moat House to Devereux Court.

Devereux Court

(21) Bodenham Lakes Nature Reserve / Bodenham Gravel Pits / Lady Close Farm (A63 / 11 / 238)

This little timber-framed farm house only stood for a short time. It was built around 1813 and by the 1950s had succumbed to the growth of the gravel pits around it. But the name, Lady Close, is much older than the farm the land being so named because in the 1540s, and probably for a long time before that, it belonged to the chantry of St Mary in Bodenham church.

The title deeds to the farm started in 1799 with the sale of a parcel of land called 'Lady Close Orchard' by Nicholas Mason of Howton to Thomas Wright. The land was described as being 'bounded on the north by the West Road'. This was the road running west out of the village, now destroyed by the gravel works (see section on roads in the village). The road is still visible as a ditch or depression that is crossed by the track entering the Bodenham Lake Nature Reserve. The house stood just to the south of this road and the position of the front door, which faced north to the road, is still marked today by two box bushes that stood on either side of the door and are now embedded in the overgrown Cupressus hedge.

The Wright family built the house and then sold the whole property to Thomas and Elizabeth Beavan whose nephew later sold it to Lot Newman of the Vern (56). Then in 1838 Lot Newman sold it to John Arkwright for £132 10s. During these proceedings Lot Newman was very ill in bed and the curate, Rev Lewes (see 23), collected the title deeds and took them to Leominster after which the lawyer hired a horse and rode over to the Vern himself to take the purchase money. But the property only remained a part of the Hampton Court estate for a short time until it was transferred to the vicar as part of the Glebe Exchange that took place when the Rev Henry Arkwright died.

Then in 1919 Lady Close, along with most of the Bodenham Glebe, was sold by auction and the property was bought by Harry Davies, though he had been asked to bid for John Baggot who lived at the Hollies (19). Davies put in a tenant but shortly after started gravel digging on the farm in a small way 'with wheelbarrows'. However he soon sold out to a larger gravel company and so the place came eventually into the hands of Redlands who extended the excavations further and further west acquiring land from Hampton Court as they required it.

As the gravel works expanded Lady Close ceased to operate as a farm and first the house and then the farm buildings were abandoned and pulled down. Gravel working reigned supreme until 1986 when, after a Public Inquiry, Redlands was forced to abandon its plans to extend over the river, moved elsewhere and eventually sold the site to Leominster District Council. In this way the site came into the ownership of the Herefordshire Council when it was first set up. The open water formed by the gravel digging attracted a great variety of birds from the start, especially Great-Crested Grebes, and the area has now been designated as a Nature Reserve. More recently still the old farm orchard has been replanted and extended with perry pears and cider apples and its name, Lady Close Orchard, preserves the original name of the land belonging to the chantry in Bodenham church.

Lady Close Farm
as seen from the top of the church tower

(22) Bodenham Cottages / The Cottage Homes

In 1898 an architect was 'walking about the village with pencil, paper and a measuring tape looking for a possible site for the Bodenham Homes' and here he must have thought he had found the ideal one, facing south and overlooking the meadows and orchards of Lady Close Farm. He could never have envisaged the noisy machinery, huge piles of gravel and gigantic lorries throwing up clouds of dust that were soon to be the main view from the Homes. Nor that, by 2002, not only would the gravel works have gone but also the inhabitants for whom the Homes were made.

The Cottage Homes were opened with a golden key on August 17th 1898 by Miss Sophia Arkwright, daughter of the late vicar in whose memory they were built. They were endowed by Miss Arkwright and her sister and were intended for 'three aged widows and a nurse who is to devote herself to supervision of the inmates and also to act as a parish nurse' the latter being something much needed in the village. Residents of Bodenham had priority and 'a male may be elected - failing the existence of females'. There were three single storied houses and one, for the nurse, with an upstairs.

Ten Rules were drawn up and a copy hung in every house. One copy of these survived and was taken to the Hereford Record Office for safe keeping but a photocopy in the original frame still hangs in the western cottage. The rules included restrictions on lodgers, pigs and poultry, forbade the accumulation of refuse and made provisions about the enforcement of cleanliness etc.

The first nurse appointed was Nurse Moore who had worked in the cholera hospital in London in 1849 when deaths averaged a thousand a week. After her came Nurse Potter who later married the organist, Mr Simpson (see 6). The appointment of a District Nurse in the area and the building of Crawshay Cottage in Bodenham Moor in 1936 meant the nurse's house here was no longer needed and the larger house was used for someone who could act as warden. The Homes were later modernised and bathrooms put in but by 1980 they were all empty and in the end were sold, the money going to build more houses beside the Siward James Homes.

After the sale the original range of outbuildings at the back were pulled down. These had provided each house with an outside lavatory, a wash-house and a coal store, all very modern when built. Only the communal ash-pit, a little brick built building, remains. (The ashes were used in the privies). The houses were then sold into separate ownership and most have since been altered, especially with the insertion of upstairs windows.

(23) Bodenham Hall / Hill House / Meredith's (B76 / 6)

The house in the early seventeenth century was a tenanted farm house occupied by Owen and Margaret Meredith. It had two barns, several other buildings and 50 acres of arable land in scattered strips in the open fields of the parish. In 1634 it was bought by William Clark of Pencombe from Hugh Walshe and then came into the ownership of the Mason family.

But evidence of an earlier house on the site comes from the presence of massive, re-used cruck timbers in the roof and a fragment of 13th-century pottery found deep in the garden soil.

By 1717 it was being called Hill House, perhaps because it was occupied by a Thomas Hill, and then in 1740 it was sold by Edward Mason to John Reece of Marden. He was described as a

Wine bottle seal from 1738

'gent' and was probably the first owner occupier of the house. His wife, Mary, was a Unett of Freens Court, Marden.

The house as it stands today is made of two timber-framed units standing at right angles to each other. The northern part is the older and is built mainly of large, re-used timbers including parts of the two crucks. This will have been the Meredith's house.

The south-facing part of the house, also timber-framed but always covered with stucco, was built later, probably by John and Mary Reece since it incorporates features more typical of a gentleman's residence than a simple farm house. John Reece had his own wine bottles and a lovely seal from one of these has been found in the garden with the inscription 'I * R 1738' embossed on it. John Reece was a gentleman farmer and he owned the Hollies or Cross Farm (19) as well from where his farming operations would have been carried out

The Reeces had two sons but both died young and they took a niece, Mary Unett, to live with them. She remained unmarried and stayed with her uncle until his death when she inherited his property. But by then the house was mortgaged and Mary Unett just got deeper and deeper into debt until she was forced to sell Bodenham Hall and move into the Hollies (19) where the rest of her life can be followed. She sold the house to an Arkwright, but unusually it was not to either Richard Arkwright or his son John but to another son, Joseph. Joseph was in holy orders and it seems probable that his father intended the Bodenham living for him. However the incumbent, the Rev Waite Robinson was long-lived. For a period he went to Cheltenham for his wife's health and Joseph came to replace him when he would have lived in the Vicarage in the field (13). It seems likely that Joseph bought Bodenham Hall as his intended Vicarage. But he never lived there. May be the hunting did not come up to expectation, for Joseph was a hunting parson said to have been the model for Trollope's Mark Robart, or perhaps his intended bride did not like the house or perhaps he was not prepared to wait for the vicar to die. Whatever the cause he sold the house to his brother John of Hampton Court and moved to Northamptonshire.

Under the Hampton Court estate the first tenant was a John Gallier who proved very unsatisfactory and was thrown out in 1822 but not before he and Miss Unett had fallen out over who was to sit in the Bodenham Hall pew in the church.

After this the house was given a thorough overhaul and the agricultural land that had gone with it was transferred to Bodenham Court Farm (31) leaving only garden, orchard, stable and coach house (24) going with the house.

The new tenants by 1823 were the Turberville family, first William with his daughter Rhoda and then, perhaps on William's death, his brother Matthew with his wife Elizabeth and several daughters. Elizabeth's sister, Rhoda Wilkins, lived over the road with her husband at the Hollies (19) so there would have been a lot of coming and going between the two households.

Rather later Rhoda Turberville married the curate, the Rev David Lewes who was acting as vicar during a second long absence of Rev. Waite Robinson at Cheltenham. They both lived at Bodenham Hall and had one daughter, Emma Georgeana. As the older Turbervilles died and the other daughters married and moved away the Lewes family remained in sole occupation of the house. David Lewes made his presence felt both in the parish and in the house, where he was always asking the agent to have things done, including having water brought to the house from the spring above (see 82).

Then the Rev Waite Robinson died and although Joseph Arkwright was no longer available there was an Arkwright of the next generation, Henry , nephew of John Arkwright of Hampton Court, who was in holy orders and he became the new vicar. It was inevitable that David Lewes, having run the parish for so long on his own, would find it hard to work under a younger man. He moved away trying to obtain a living elsewhere but, failing in this and probably thanks to the kindness of John Arkwright, he returned to live at Bodenham Hall as a clergyman 'without care of souls' until his death in 1868.

His widow and daughter, having been left the Hollies by Rhoda Wilkins, then moved across the road to live there, just as Mary Unett had done before them and the house continued to be occupied by curates, five in all, serving under the Rev Henry Arkwright.

Henry Arkwright died in 1889 and his successor, Rev Sturges, unable to live in Henry Arkwright's huge vicarage (55) spent a year in Bodenham Hall while his new vicarage (39) was being altered for him. After he left the curates returned, at least four of them in succession. It is not surprising that at least two people have reported seeing the ghosts of clergymen about the house, probably the Rev David Lewes still keeping an eye on the place.

By 1905 the curates were gone and the house was let to William Price, a retired farmer from the Vern (56) and a churchwarden. About this time the name of the house was changed to Bodenham Hall. In other parts of the country the name 'Hall' takes the place of 'Court' ie the place where the manorial court was held, which in Bodenham was Devereux Court (20). The use of the name here, being recent, carries no such implications.

At the estate sale in 1923 the house was sold to Major C.T. Jones M.F.H. and later to Mrs Nott. The coach house was subsequently made into a separate dwelling and the house itself was divided into two houses.

It is tempting to think that this house stands near what may have been the earliest site in the village to have been occupied. The Ladywell (82B), with its abundant supply of water, is just above the house and in the orchard around are numerous flat areas that look very like ancient house platforms. The area would certainly repay investigation.

(24) The Coach House / Bodenham Hall Cottages

This building was probably built around 1740 by John Reece as a coach house to serve Bodenham Hall (23) or Hill House as it was then called. It was open to the roof at the north end and had a stable and saddle room at the south end. Its connection with Bodenham Hall is shown by the ashlared stone wall facing west towards the house and not as might have been expected east towards Ladywell Lane.

The building was sold with Bodenham Hall to the Arkwrights in 1818 and then, in 1851 was converted to a 'double cottage' which involved fairly major structural alterations. The two cottages were occupied first by a gamekeeper and a shop keeper and then by workmen involved in building the second Dinmore tunnel. In 1892 Mr Arkwright allowed the curate, Rev Garnons Williams, then living at Bodenham Hall, to convert one of the cottages into a 'Reading and Recreation Room'. This was on the first floor at the north end of the building and was reached by a staircase from an entrance, now blocked up, opening on to Ladywell Lane. All sorts of activities went on here including whist matches and suppers but by 1921 these were becoming less popular and 'the old Reading Room was converted for a carpentry workshop and cookery room for the school'.

At the 1923 sale most of the building was sold with Bodenham Hall and the new owner persuaded the Vicar to exchange the Reading Room for a wooden shed provided near the school for the carpentry. For the next 50 years or so the building served as a double garage for Bodenham Hall with a cottage at the south end.

(25) Barrs Cottage / Ladywell Lane Cottage / The Bank / Bunhill / Watkin's

This cottage, the lower of the two that used to stand up Ladywell Lane, was a part of the Hampton Court estate when Richard Arkwright bought it in 1810 and at that time had 4 acres of arable land with it. The name Barrs Cottage refers to the field on the edge of which the cottage stood. The tenant was John Watkins but it is probable that he was formerly the owner. In 1810 he gave up the cottage and entered Coningsby Hospital which implies that he was either an old soldier or one time servant at Hampton Court.

After Watkins left 'the old cottage and barn' was converted into two cottages and the 4 acres was probably added to Bodenham Court Farm. The northern of the two cottages was occupied by Thomas Yeoman, a stonemason and son of Richard Yeoman (27). The last family to live there were Mrs Acton, a war widow, and her two sons, one of whom later described the cottage as being timber-frame with brick infill. They had a pigsty, garden and orchard with two or three large Walnut trees and a Pear tree. They got their water from the Ladywell (82) by the lane just below and it was 'a proper spring with an arched top'.

The cottage was not nearly as isolated then as now. The baker came twice a week on his way to the Henhouse (52), on weekdays men walked that way to Hampton Court to work and on fine Sundays people would come up from the village for an afternoon stroll. Mr Acton remembered being taken as a boy to gather wild daffodils in the woods above to decorate the church at Easter and to Hampton Court to pay the rent. After the 1923 estate sale the rent had to be taken to Bodenham Manor (55), the new owners, instead and he did not like going there: 'they were frightening with monks in robes all round' (actually some kind of sect).

The southern cottage was occupied for a long period by Thomas Gatehouse, a gardener at Hampton Court. By the 1920s both houses were empty and derelict and were used on occasion by the Brownies (see 26). They then disappeared under bushes. But in 1982 the boys at Bodenham Manor school carried out an excavation on the site. They found that the original cottage had been at the north end and the barn at the south and brought to light a lot of broken china and several small domestic items.

(26) Top Ladywell Lane Cottage / Bunhill Cottage / William Bailey's Cottage

This stone cottage with thatched roof stood at the top of Ladywell Lane where it joined the main track up to the Henhouse (52). In 1793 it belonged to John Lawrence of Felton whose family sold it to Richard Yeoman of the New Inn (27). He gave it to Richard Arkwright in exchange for Churchwalk Cottage (6) when it was described as 'cottage, outbuildings and garden with half an acre of land'. It needed a thorough overhaul, its walls were giving way and had to be buttressed at one end. It only had a ladder to reach the upper floor but there is no mention of making a staircase. At first it was occupied by agricultural workers but then by James Newman, son of Lot Newman of the Vern (56) who was promoted to estate gamekeeper. He had five sons who all presumably climbed the ladder to bed each night.

At the 1923 sale the cottage was bought by Mrs Medlicot of Bodenham Court Farm (31) and Fred Williams the stockman was the last person to live there. He used to take down an empty bucket every morning to get drinking water from the Cross Well and carry it back up full at lunch time. Not surprising that later he moved down to Pease Green(15). After this the house was bought by the ffrench-Davies family of Bodenham Manor (55) and for a short time it came to life again when the Guides moved in as described and illustrated in their Log Book of 1927. There were eight guides in two patrols—Lily-of-the-valley and Forget-me-not:

Drawing of the cottage by one of the Guides

We had no club room ... but later on Lieutenant's mother, Mrs ffrench-Davies, very kindly gave us the use of one of her empty cottages...it had four little rooms and a lovely garden and an orchard and a paddock. We were excited and made haste to make furniture and move in ...

Some of us brought curtains, one a table, others brushes, fire-arms, pictures etc. We got round blocks of wood and painted them and inscribed them with our names for seats. Each patrol chose a corner and decorated it and soon the room had a very Guide-y and home-like air.

(27 & 28) Garden of the Coach House / The New Inn & New Inn Cottages (B76, Box 14)

The New Inn and the cottages no longer exist but their site is known and the deeds give information about the properties back to 1700. At that time the property was owned by Francis Brace and then by Ann Hughes. It then passed to the Gibbons family—several generations, all called William.

The first William Gibbons (William Gibbons I), had acquired land in Great Bunhill Field close by in 1738 and it was his son William Gibbons (II), a tailor, who bought the house from Ann Hughes when it was described as: 'messuage, fold, garden, barn, beast house, stable and outhouse'.

Arable land was included in the sale so it was in fact a small farm and William Gibbons (III) seems to have become fairly prosperous leaving several legacies when he died. His son, William (IV), married and had one son (William V) but then died young, leaving Miss Mary Unett of Bodenham Hall (23) as trustee of his will. His widow Hester had a hard time making ends meet and in 1809 wrote to the overseers of the poor to say they must find somewhere for her father, who lived with her, as she was going to let her house and go into service. But in the event she remained in the house and remarried, this time a stonemason called Richard Yeoman, and he and Hester had six children two being boys who, with their step-brother William, were all trained as stonemasons.

When William Gibbons (V) came of age he sold the house to his step-father. Richard Yeomans then paid off the legacies still owing from the will of William (III) and built two cottages on the land. One was probably made from the barn but the other was made new, a bit further up Ladywell Lane. He made the original house into an inn called the New Inn. He still continued to work as a stonemason and built at least two other houses in the village (6 and 71).

Richard Yeoman's main legacy to the village however was the tall stone, now much worn away, that still stands on the Green in the medieval socket stone. The vicar writing in the parish magazine in 1923 described how the stone was brought from Dudales Hope quarry in the 1840s and set in the old socket stone. It was tall, hexagonal in section and came to a sharp point at the top (see 81).

Richard Yeoman died in 1902 but Hester continued to run the pub with the help of a barmaid. All the children moved away except Thomas who, still a stonemason, lived first at Belle Ville (5) and then at Barrs Cottage (25). He had three boys and inevitably one was called William.

One of the cottages was occupied by Mary Wilson, a 'garden woman' aged 74 at the time of the 1861 census and too deaf to hear the census enumerator and say where she was born, or perhaps she did not wish to say.

In 1866 Mr Arkwright bought the whole property described then as 'messuage with stable, cider mill and two cottages' for £500. It was so dilapidated that all the buildings were taken down and the stones used to build the wall beside Ladywell Lane opposite the Coach House (24). The northern part of the land was added to Bodenham Court Farm (31) land and the southern part became a part of the garden of Bodenham Hall (23).

There are few signs today of all the buildings that once stood on the site, of the large family that lived there or of all the comings and goings of a village pub but a great deal of broken pottery and bits of broken clay pipes have been found here.

(29) 'The Old Oast House' / Hop Kiln at Bodenham Court Farm / Building at Devereux Court

This building, lying to the north of Bodenham Court Farm (31) is timber-framed in construction but now has stone walls on two sides. It is of two stories and (in 1980) had two round holes visible in the ceiling of the ground floor. This was where the long hop pockets were hung so that the dried hops could be shovelled in from above. To pack the hops tightly a man wearing a large hat, would jump down into the empty pocket and then, as the hops were shovelled in from above, would tread them down firmly gradually rising up as the pocket filled till he could walk out at the top and the tightly packed pocket was ready to be sewn up.

Hops were last grown on Bodenham Court Farm in the Medlicot's time but a cowl was still in place on the east end of the roof in 1938 though the kiln itself had gone. However it had been active all through the 19th century as shown by the records of frequent repairs.

The hop kiln was part of Bodenham Court Farm for a hundred years or so but the building itself is much older. Its appearance at Bodenham Court Farm is precisely dated by the estate Building Records which in 1823 describe: 'taking down the Hop Kiln at Devereux Court and rebuilding it at Bodenham Court Farm'. The total cost was £120 - 18s - 5d and the move took place in January.

The history of the building before the move is not so certain. It had certainly been used as a hop kiln at Devereux Court (26) before it was moved but mouldings on the central truss were identified by a local expert as being typical of a building of the fourteenth century. These mouldings are on one side of the beam only and this indicates that it had been an open hall house with moulding on the 'high side' of the room only where the lord of the manor and his lady would have sat. Since the present Devereux Court is said to be fifteenth century and since this building that probably predates it had stood, before it was moved, close by it seems possible that this was the earlier Devereux Court. The building has now been made into a house.

(30) Well Cottage / Crosswell Cottage / The Gables / Jays Bank Farm ? / The Vineyard ?

From 1828 onwards the history of this house is well documented. It belonged to the Hampton Court estate and was occupied over a long period by the Reynolds family. At first John Reynolds was the tenant of only part of the cottage and two aged women lived in the other part. Considering this arrangement the agent commented that the house was: 'large enough for a double labourer's cottage but the garden ground would be too confined and it is probably better let as at present than incur the expense of alteration'. This remark shows the importance attributed by the Arkwrights to a good vegetable garden for all their tenants and accounts for the large gardens that Bodenham houses still have today.

Mary Reynolds, who died in 1925 aged 92, had lived in the house a long time and told the vicar her own memories of Bodenham as well as those she had heard from her parents-in-law. She described how on certain days people used to gather on the village green (see 81) in front of the house sitting around on large stones that lay about with baskets of produce for sale. Was this a survival from the days when Bodenham had a weekly market the licence for which had been granted to Walter Devereux in 1378?

Before 1828 the history of the house is not so clear. The problem is, that although on structural features the house has been dated to the sixteenth or seventeenth century it is not marked on the Enclosure map of 1813 which elsewhere has proved to be very accurate. One reason for this apparent omission could be that, like the Old Hopkiln (29), the house had been moved to its present site from elsewhere after 1813.

There is evidence to show that this was indeed the case. In the Building Records 'Reynold's Cottage' is sometimes referred to as 'late Jays' or 'formerly Jays' and in the pew list Richard Arkwright is recorded as paying for a pew for 'Jays Bank Farm', as part of the Hampton Court estate. The property listed in the estate sale catalogue that best fits this name is a house described as 'The Vinyard ... tenant James Jay. late Earl of Essex'. This indicates that Arkwright had bought Jays Bank

Well Cottage

Farm in the 1808 sale as a part of the estate under the name of the Vinyard.

A list of houses of the same date gives 'The Vinyard' as lying between Bodenham Hall (23) and Bodenham Court Farm (31). Since a house called The Vinyard existed in 1808 it should be marked on the Enclosure map and although there is no building on the site of today's Well Cottage there is indeed a building between Bodenham Hall and Bodenham Court Farm standing well back from the road.

This makes it very probable that The Vinyard and Well Cottage are one and the same building which was moved some time between 1813 and 1820 when the Arkwright's Building Record Books start. The move was probably associated with the big changes taking place at Bodenham Court Farm at about that time.

Such a move would also account for the way that Well Cottage is rather awkwardly placed on a sharp corner and out of line with the other buildings to the north of the road. The house may even have encroached onto the village green. Other indications that the house was moved include signs in the timber-frame structure of the house showing that alterations have taken place and the initials 'JW' which are carved just near the front door. These could stand for John Wanklin, a carpenter / builder who was known to have been working in the village at that time.

In more recent times the house has had many name changes; from Well Cottage to Crosswell Cottage to The Gables and back to Well Cottage again.

(31) Bodenham Court / Bodenham Court Farm / Corbetts Farm

This house occupies an important site in the village standing as it does close to the village green (81) and Cross Well and it was the last working farm in the village until it too was sold without its land in the 1990s.

In the eighteenth century there were eight or more farms with their farm houses situated along the main road through the village and this one was probably no larger than the others. But, unlike the others, it had been associated with the Devereux family for a long time and this association has led to a confusion over names. Any mention of 'Bodenham Court' or simply 'the Court' up to the end of the nineteenth century was almost certainly referring to the ancient manorial house of Devereux Court (20) but from about 1810 onwards the same names would have been referring to what is now Bodenham Court Farm (31). The name, Bodenham Court Farm, really means what it says, ie that it was the farm and buildings associated with the Court House of Bodenham which was Devereux Court and not a farm called Bodenham Court which might indicate a second manor in the village.

The main wing of the house which faces south was probably built in the seventeenth century but there have been many fairly radical alterations especially to the roof and the south front and a new wing added. It seems that the house may have had a thorough upgrading around 1800 and that is just the period when the name 'Bodenham Court Farm' begins to appear in documents. Significantly however no early title deeds under that name have been found.

Instead about that time a property called 'Corbetts Farm', which had figured in many earlier deeds, ceased to be mentioned and it seems probable that the two houses, 'Bodenham Court Farm' and 'Corbetts Farm' were in fact the same place which had just changed its name.

This conclusion is born out by the fact that in the 1807 Land Tax returns Mr Thomas West was named as renting 'Corbetts Farm' from the Earl of Essex (Coningsby) while other records of the same period name Mr Thomas West as the tenant of 'Bodenham Court Farm'. Assuming this change in name to be correct then the earlier history of Bodenham Court Farm must be looked for under the name of Corbetts Farm.

The earliest record found for Corbetts Farm is a 1611 lease from the Earl of Essex (Devereux) to one Thomas Vicar of London, a salter. With Corbetts Farm was leased the Woodhouse (75) and the mill on the Lugg (81) but no hint is given of just where Corbetts Farm stood. Later leases show the same three properties owned by the Marquis of Bath so it is clear that they were a part of the ancient Devereux inheritance in Bodenham. With Devereux Court they were sold to the Earl of Essex (Conyngsby) in 1803. This is confirmed by the land tax records for 1807 which show that 'Corbetts Farm, Woodhouse and Lugg Mill' were at that date owned by the Earl of Essex and thus a part of the Hampton Court estate.

Devereux Court had become very run down by this date and the long-established tenant, James Newton had died in 1802 so when the estate was sold in the following year this seems to have led to a reversal of roles. Devereux Court, now much dilapidated, was divided up into four cottages while Corbetts Farm was modernised and enlarged for a new tenant and came to be known as 'Bodenham Court Farm'.

But the Arkwright's building records show that in 1813, though the house itself had probably been enlarged, there were few farm buildings and providing these was the next step in moving the working centre of the demesne farm from Devereux Court (20) and the Old Parsonage farm (1) up to Bodenham Court Farm (31). The first buildings to be moved were the two tithe barns (2) and this may have involved moving Well Cottage (30) out of the way first. Sadly the estate building records had not started properly by this date. But the moving of the next building, the old hop-kiln, up from Devereux Court was fully documented as described under (29). More additions to the farm buildings followed soon after but these were all built new or made out of existing buildings standing on the site. The most important of these additions were as follows:

1829	New cattle shed and fence walls, 1830 Making a new cart stable out of a shed and increasing cart stable. Making pig sties out of old cart stable, altering doors of Hackney stable.
1839	Building calves cot 1853 Taking down old building, building cowhouse and stable.
1876	Taking down old buildings. New carthorse stable.

Other buildings—machine house, calves cot, pigsties, cider mill shed, granary, poultry shed, duck's cot and several more—are all mentioned.

Thomas West was tenant and was followed by his brother Joseph and then by John Hill. In 1831 John Colebourne became tenant and in his time water was brought to the farm. His son did not follow him in the tenancy (see 8) and so after him came Henry Medlicot whose large family played an important role in the village in the following years. At some time in all these changes Mr Arkwright found the church's fourteenth-century font in the farmyard being used as a drinking trough and had it returned to the church.

Jim Medlicot, one of Henry's sons bought the farm in the 1923 sale but in 1937 he sold it back to the Hampton Court estate, by then owned by Lady Hereford, and Mr Jack Weyman Jones took on the tenancy. He moved to Bodenham from Bosbury and many of his animals made the move on foot. He was a notable breeder of Hereford cattle and many of his memories, recounted after he had retired to the Hollies(19), are incorporated into this account of the village.

(32) Pump Cottage (A63/ I I / 229)

The title deeds to this stone built cottage start in 1731 but give the earlier information that Thomas Cheese, a glover who had formerly lived in the village, had mortgaged the house where his son Edward was living. In 1777 Edward's son John Cheese sold the house to William Hall who was a cooper and the first of three generations of William Halls to own the property. William Hall also owned the car park site (7), then a garden, and arable land in Bodenham's open fields. The second William Hall was a baker and the third a shopkeeper, though perhaps not a very successful one for he sold the property to Thomas Tirbutt of Riffins Mill (Bowley Township) and went to live at Witchill (46). However at the sale he retained 'a slang or langet (four yards wide) which has a small cottage erected on it at the end thereof next the road'. This was occupied by his mother Mary and was probably built for her when her husband died as what would be called a 'granny flat' today.

Soon after this both the main house and Mary Hall's cottage were sold to the Hampton Court estate. Mary Hall died in 1855 and her cottage was then taken down but the flat area on which it had stood is still visible. An 'old barn' going with the house itself was also taken down and the stone used to build the wall beside the road. This barn was probably used by the first William Hall to house the crops from his land in the open fields and shows that this cottage was once a small, part-time farm. After this the house was occupied by agricultural workers employed on the estate.

(33) Goode's Cottage / Meyrick's Cottage (B76 / Box I3)

Built in the seventeenth century this timber-framed cottage with a large stone chimney was originally thatched though later the thatch was replaced by corrugated iron. It had one storey and an attic and sadly was demolished in the 1960s to be replaced, on a slightly different site, by the two semi-detached brick houses that stand there today. The title deeds only start around 1800 when the cottage was bought by Edward Loton, a yeoman. It had formerly been occupied by John Hall a cooper and possibly brother of William Hall next door. Edward Loton died in 1809 and left the cottage to his friend, John Meyrick. According to his inventory his most valuable possession was his watch and his only furniture his bed. No doubt other items had been moved before the assessors arrived.

John Meyrick moved in to live there. Twenty years later he was in financial difficulties and first made the cottage into two dwellings and then sold it to the Hampton Court estate. As was usual in these sales to the estate he would have been allowed to remain for his life but he actually moved away from Bodenham to live with his daughter in Pencombe. John Reynolds, an agricultural worker probably on the estate, then moved in.

Goode's Cottage / Meyrick's Cottage

In 1829 when the stone wall in front of Pump Cottage was built it was continued in front of this cottage too and steps and gateposts were put in. The position of this entrance is still visible in the wall today.

The Goodes were the last people to live in the cottage when Bill Goode worked for Mr Weyman Jones at Bodenham Court Farm. They did not want to leave the cottage and move into one of the new houses. Mrs Goode complained that there was less room there than in the old cottage.

(34) Vicarage Cottages (A63 / 11 / 240)

The deeds for this property give information well back into the eighteenth century but the house must be much older because crucks are incorporated into the structure. The first known owner was Thomas Hayes who was a rope-maker. The 1813 Enclosure map shows a building behind the house which was as long as the tithe barns but narrower. This was parallel with the road. No barn is ever mentioned with the house so this building may have been a covered rope-walk. Here Thomas Hayes would have laid out the long strands of hemp which were then twisted to make into rope. Thomas Hayes' son was probably also a rope-maker.

He married the daughter of a joiner and their daughter seems to have gone up in the world when she married Samuel Yate Esq. The Yates' son inherited the property but sold it, without its land to the tenant, Thomas Hope, a weaver. After him came John Hare, a shopkeeper but he got into financial troubles, let off a part of the house and started a series of mortgages. An insurance policy at this time describes the property as 'two cottages, shed and outbuildings, stone, timber, lath and plaster, tiled and thatched'.

Then in 1840 John Hare sold the house to the Hampton Court estate and, as always, they allowed him to stay till he died and then gave it a thorough repair with alterations to make it into two dwellings. It sounds as though, although two families had lived in the house for thirty years, no alterations to facilitate this had been made before. One of the two cottages was let to a farm worker and the other remained a shop at first, run by Catherine Chamberlain and was then let to a wheel-wright, William Pierce. The constant presence of craftsmen in this cottage indicates that the 'sheds and outhouses' were workshops.

In 1862 William Pierce asked that a 'fence' in his garden should be shifted further from his door but a pencil note by the agent refused because 'the fence was put there by order of the late Mr Arkwright'. This shows the detailed interest that the Arkwrights took in their tenants and proper-ties. The 'fence', made of stone slabs, is still there, rather awkwardly placed dividing the front gardens on a different line from the division between the houses.

Following the death of Rev Henry Arkwright and the move of the new vicar, Rev Sturges, to the Old Vicarage (39) there was a glebe exchange and these two cottages became a part of the new glebe. After this the eastern cottage, the one nearest the vicarage, was occupied by the parish clerk, sexton and verger until about 1965 when the cottages were sold into private ownership.

(35) The Retreat / Hurst View Cottage (A63 / 11 / 227)

This timber framed cottage is said to have been built in the seventeenth century. Together with Hurst View (36) it was a part of the Hampton Court estate when Richard Arkwright bought it in 1810. The cottage, with half an acre of land, was occupied then by William Mytton and the estate spent £20 on alterations. William Mytton was given notice to quit 'having been detected stealing part of a hedge at the Henhouse' (52) but the threat, as always, was never carried out and later he moved down to Church House (4).

Then in 1837 Richard Arkwright gave the property together with Hurst View (36) next door to Hugh and Ann Gladding in exchange for the cottage south of the Old P.O. (8). Thereafter it was known as Hurst View cottage but around 1935 was sold to Mr Jack Weyman Jones of Bodenham Court Farm (31) for one of his men to live in. It was of two rooms downstairs with an attic lit from the gables but has subsequently been enlarged and changed its name again.

(36) Hurst View / The Retreat / Gladwin Villa / The Redhouse? (A63 / 11 / 227)

This house has had more confusing name changes than any other in the village. The house, together with the Retreat (35) next door was a part of the Hampton Court estate when Richard Arkwright bought it in 1810. It was occupied then by Elizabeth Harris a widow and after by her son John, a waggoner. Then in 1820 Richard Arkwright gave the property to Hugh Gladding in exchange for some land near the Henhouse (53) and he on his death left this and the house next door (35) to his son William Gladding who was head carpenter on the Hampton Court estate in charge of the wood-lands. The Gladdings, father and son both lived in Hope so had tenants in the house.

The 1813 map shows this house as no larger than The Retreat (35) next door and it seems prob-able that it was the Gladdings who enlarged it and upgraded it with Tudor revival windows and perhaps called it Gladwin Villa after their own name. The upgrading may have included putting rough-cast over a brick building causing a change of name from the Red House. After this the house went up in the world and was occupied by the Davies family who employed a servant and changed the name to The Retreat. Then the house was taken over by the Bodenham doctors starting with Dr Newman who moved across the road from the Old Vicarage (39). Doctors lived here up to 1940 as part of a Hereford practice and even after it was sold one room was retained as the Surgery. Today after almost 100 years of medical history the only remaining sign is the 'S' of Surgery over one door and this will soon be gone.

(37) The Village (B76/Box 1 / Bundle 36)

It is not really known how this house acquired its unusual name but in the nineteenth century few Bodenham houses had individual names most being known just by the name of the family that lived there. As a result in the 1861 census houses along the main road through the village were all described on the form just as 'Village' as opposed to those in 'Pease Green' near the church and those called 'Chapel' by the bridge, so perhaps this name stuck just for this one house.

A Thomas White lived here in 1813 and was probably keeping a shop among other things for in 1818 the parish clerk recorded: 'paid Mr White 4s 6d for a broom for the church'. Thomas White was probably a man of some substance, owning his house and being called 'Mr' and it was almost certainly he who built Bunhill Villa (40), perhaps as a speculation.

In 1829 both these houses were sold to Thomas Symonds of Stoke Prior and shortly after, in 1836 were put up for auction when The Village was bought by the Hampton Court estate. At that time it was described as a large house with five bedrooms and shop with two bow windows (as it has today) and an extensive range of buildings including a barn, which indicates that it had been run at least partly as a farm

Under the Arkwrights the property was occupied first by a cordwainer and then by a skilled stonemason, William Mason, who made a new font for Leominster priory. He worked for the Hampton Court estate and helped to build the new Vicarage in Bodenham (55). However by 1857 he was being described as just a shopkeeper.

The last person to keep shop here was Miss Mary Jane Baggot a 'grocer and farmer' who later moved to the Hollies (19).

(38) The Pigeon House / Fordham House

Piecing together the early history of this large house has been hampered by the absence of earlier deeds but the R.C.H.M. say that the house was built in the eighteenth century. The pigeon house or dovecot itself was probably of the same date and definitely built after 1761 when an Act of Parliament removed earlier regulations restricting the ownership of pigeon houses to the Lord of the Manor.

It is possible that the eighteenth-century house was built by the Sirrel family of Wistaston Court, Marden and in the early nineteenth century it was occupied by Nicholas Sirrel's daughter, Mary, and her husband Rev Thomas Wynne. Mary's sister lived just over the road at the Old Vicarage (39). Two children were born to the Wynne's in Bodenham, both christened by their father though he was not the vicar.

In 1850 the house was sold to the Arkwrights and underwent extensive alterations especially at the eastern end which was pulled down and rebuilt, this has left the vertical line visible in the brickwork of the north wall.

The cellars were deepened and a lot of work was done on the outbuildings, stables, cow house etc which probably stood at the west end. A fine garden was planted including cherries, nectarines, apricots and greengages. Various tenants occupied the re-furbished house, one of whom gave it the name of Fordham House.

Then in 1913 the house, together with Tan-y-Bryn (17) where the gardener lived, was sold by the Arkwrights to Mr R.Crawshay Bailey, an ironworks owner whose family had lived at Little Hereford. It was very unusual at that time for the Hampton Court estate to sell any properties which suggests perhaps that Mr Arkwright and Mr Bailey were friends. The earlier title deeds were probably handed over to Mr Bailey at this time which would explain why they have not been found in the Hampton Court archives. But if so they were subsequently lost for they were not available when the house was sold recently.

Mr Bailey added to the house at the western end, perhaps removing a stable and cow house in the process. He was a churchwarden and strong supporter of the church and when his first wife died he gave the two stained glass windows in the south aisle of the church in her memory. The second Mrs Bailey was very active in village affairs.

The Bailey tombstone in the churchyard is very distinctive and one of Mr Bailey's sons, Richard, is buried there too. He was a schoolmaster and was said to have turned down the headship of Eton College in favour of Quarry Bank School, Liverpool, famous now as the school attended by the Beatles. Another pupil was the actor David Nimmo who described Mr Bailey as 'a remarkable man - a visionary head'. Richard Bailey used to bring small groups of the boys to stay in Bodenham for a few days before setting off down the Lugg on 'a skiff'. These excursions are still remembered with affection by his past pupils and sometimes a small wreath from Quarry Bank appears beside the Bailey grave stone in the churchyard.

The Dovecot

(38a) Outhouse at the Pigeon House / Pound Cottage

Part of this building still stands beside the road just to the northeast of the Pigeon House. In 1931 more of the building was present and though being used as a store at that time it had clearly formerly been a cottage and was said by the RCHM to have been built in the seventeenth century. It was a two-storied, timber-framed building of three bays with a roof of stone slates, the upper storey having no windows.

Documentary evidence shows that this was a cottage known as Pound Cottage and owned in 1806 by the Earl of Essex (Coningsby). It was occupied by a John Powell with 20 perches of arable in the open fields. Being a part of the Hampton Court estate it was sold to the Arkwrights but soon after Richard Arkwright exchanged various properties with Nicholas Sirrell who received this cottage occupied then by Ann Powell, a widow, as his share of the proceedings. Since then it has always been a part of the Pigeon House property.

Outhouse at the Pigeon House / Pound Cottage

(39) The Old Vicarage / The Vicarage / The Lawns / The Penthouse (A63 / II / 239)

The deeds to this house, or 'writings' as they were called, start in 1599 when Thomas Harley of Brampton Bryan sold 'a messuage with croft adjacent' to John Tyrer of Marden, a yeoman. This passed by marriage to the Jenkins family who in 1701 sold it to Daniel Wright, a blacksmith, whose father (Thomas Wright I) lived at Bridge Cottages (42 & 43).

The Wright family were moving up in the world and when Daniel's son, Thomas (II) married Mary Newton of Devereux Court (20) his 'smith's shop' was included in the marriage settlement. Thomas Wright (II) was described as a yeoman farmer and on his death his inventory included:

6 working oxen, 25 cows, 11 store beasts, 4 horses, 2 colts, 40 sheep, 20 pigs with £20 worth of hops, unsold, grain in the barn and wheat and cheese in the garret.

But there is no mention of the smith's shop or tools so perhaps this had already been sold.

Thomas's widow moved down to Bridge Cottages and her son, Thomas (III), with his wife Grace lived in the house which in these days was always called 'the Penthouse'. The reason for the name is not known but presumably the house had a pentice or sloping roof attached to the main building at some time. This was probably to do with the smithy and would have been a place where the horses stood under cover to be shod.

As well as owning this house and farm Thomas and Grace rented the Parsonage Farm (1) and the Tithe Barns (2) but sadly Thomas fell sick and died after a long illness as his epitaph in the churchyard records:

A lingering sickness did me seize
And no physician could me ease

I sought means but all in vain
Till God did free me from pain.

Grace continued farming with their son, Thomas (IV) but he soon got into financial trouble, mortgaged the house and Bridge cottages and was later described as a butcher. Then in 1822 he sold the Penthouse and moved to live in a part of Bank House (41), where he was the 'Pound Keeper' (79), and later moved to the Old Post Office (9) where his story can be followed.

From then on the house ceased to be a farmhouse and was upgraded to a gentleman's residence. The new owner was Henry Pit Esq of Rosemaund whose wife, Ann, was sister to the wife of Rev Thomas Wynne living at the Pigeon House (38) just over the road. Henry Pitt was said the have 'rebuilt' the house. What that involved is not recorded but when he died in 1839 the inventory with his will shows that it had become quite a grand house.

Never the less when it was subsequently sold to John Arkwright he at once set about 'rebuilding the house, and building a coach house and stables'. To facilitate this a quarry was opened up on Bunhill just above and the whole works, carried out by the estate staff, took over two years to complete. Despite these extensive alterations some parts of the Wright's house seem still to remain.

The first occupant of the refurbished house was Henry Arkwright, the new, young vicar, nephew to John Arkwright. But despite the new grandeur of the house it was only to be a temporary home for the vicar while the official new Vicarage (55) was being built and it was still referred to as the 'Penthouse'. Some of Henry Arkwright's large family were born in this house but his first wife also died here. In 1847 he moved up to his permanent home with his new, second wife.

After a brief interval, during which Mary Wilson 'was paid to air and look after the house', it was occupied by a succession of doctors, John Woodyatt (see 19), Samuel Staniland, W. Baldock Fry and C. Newman, one of whom changed the name of the house to The Lawns.

Dr Newman left just at the time that the Rev Henry Arkwright died. The new vicar, the Rev H.C. Sturges, could not possibly afford to live in the huge new Vicarage and so a glebe exchange between the church and the Hampton Court estate was arranged. This involved quite a lot of land but the most important change was that the Penthouse once more became the Vicarage, but officially this time—and so, after a brief sojourn at Bodenham Hall (23), the Rev Sturges and his family moved in. Rev Sturges was a keen photographer of local scenes and started a parish magazine in which he recorded some of Bodenham's history as well as ongoing events.

After him four subsequent vicars lived in the house; Mr Paterson, Mr Worsey, Mr Gibson and Mr Thursby Pelham whose wife was the daughter of Rev. Sturgess. Photographs of these vicars hang in the church vestry.

But now this house, in its turn, was considered too large for a vicarage and so it was sold by the church in 1964 and a smaller, new Vicarage was built in a part of the garden. As a result of all these changes Bodenham has four buildings still standing in the village that have all been vicarages.

(40) Bunhill Villa (B76 / Box 13) **(25 & 36)**

This house was built between 1813 and 1829 at which time it was described as 'a newly erected messuage'. The land on which the house was built was taken out of Great Bunhill Field, one of Bodenham's open arable fields, and until 1844 the new house stood beside what was then one of the main roads out of the village (see section 83 on roads). The house was built, perhaps as a speculation, by Thomas White who lived at the Village (37) and he sold it to Thomas Symonds in 1829. Eight years later, when Thomas Symonds died, both houses were put up for auction at which time Bunhill Villa was described as: 'new built freehold house, 4 bedrooms, kitchen, parlour, back kitchen, cellar, brewhouse and dairy with 2 acres of meadow and hopland planted with fruit trees'.

The house was bought by George Perkins, mortgaged and then sold again in 1839, this time to the Hampton Court estate. After this it was occupied for a time by Nicholas Thomas the Hampton Court coachman. He died following an accident when it was reported that he was: 'thrown out of a cart at the Cross Well in Bodenham from which he received injuries which terminated his life aged 65'. An accident with a cart seems rather an ignominious end for the Estate coachman but he was probably not the first and certainly not the last person to take the corner at the Cross Well far too fast.

Later the house was occupied by James Davies, known as 'Gardener Davies' who was head gardener at Bodenham Manor (55) for Lady King-King and who in 1894 became a very voluble member of Bodenham's first Parish Council. His great interest was in footpaths which he wanted to be all paved with stone. He started with the path from Bodenham Bridge towards the Moor (now BM 12) where there are stones today but there is some evidence that these stones were there before his time as the field was called 'stepping stones plock' and on an early map it was marked as a road. At a later date, when Percy Davies lived at the house, the yellow 'Nell Gwynne' buses were garaged in a shed behind and for many years after the adjacent field was known as 'Bus-station Field'.

(41) Bank House / Caswalls Farm & Smiths Farm (AL5/II / 192 - 196 and A63 / III / 87)

This site today is occupied by Bank House, which is old and timber-framed, and the modern house called Lindale (see 45). Two quite separate sets of early deeds also refer to two houses but these were called 'Caswalls Farm' and 'Smiths Farm' and these are shown on the 1813 enclosure map together with another building which may have been a barn.

One of these two sets of documents is a bundle of title deeds covering the period 1610–1710 at which date the property was sold to Lord Coningsby and thus became a part of the Hampton Court estate. This property was known as 'Smiths Farm'.

The other set of documents is a series of leases the first of which was granted by Fitzwilliam Conningsby of Hampton Court in 1663. This was a lease to a property called 'Caswalls Farm'. The history of these two houses will be considered separately first and then it will be shown how they probably came together.

Smiths Farm

This property was always described in the deeds as 'messuage, shoppe, barn, backside, fould, garden and orchard' which 'extended to the highway leading to Bodenham Bridge on the south side'. What sort of 'shoppe' was involved is not stated but it was probably some sort of work shop rather than a place selling goods.

In 1619 this property was sold by Richard and Alice Bowker to John Hooper, gent, who in 1642 gave it to his step-daughter, Susan Smith. (John Hooper himself was probably living next door at Caswalls Farm).

The house is referred to next in a marriage settlement concerning the said Susan Smith and one Richard Beck and the description of the property is just the same except that there was now also 'a dove or pigeon house lately erected'. This was probably of timber-frame construction and has left no trace.

In 1660 Susan Beck, now a widow, gave the house to John and Elizabeth Smith, presumably her relatives, who in 1667 gave it to Thomas Smith, their son, on the occasion of his marriage to Averyl Harvey. More than forty years later in 1710 Averyl Smith, now herself a widow, with her son Thomas sold the property to Lord Coningsby and so it became a part of the Hampton Court estate.

Just before the sale in 1708 an entry in the Bodenham manorial court rolls throws an interesting light on agricultural practices at that time:

> it was agreed that the owners and occupiers of Smiths farm shall for ever allow one ridge of land in ye Little Bunhill field ... for a constant way for all people that have occasion to make use thereof and that in lieu therof ye owners and occupiers of ye said Smiths farm shall always have and take to their own use without any molestation of ye inhabitants of this manor all such grass as shall grow upon ye said lower way and we do lay a pain (fine) of 20 shillings on each person that shall at any time molest and disturb ye owners and occupiers of ye said Smiths farm in the quiet enjoyment of the said grass.

Bunhill was the large open arable field on the hillside above which was owned in strips each strip being ploughed so that it made a 'ridge'. The 'way' made out of the strip was probably what is now the track to the Bunhill Barn (58) and the complex of modern farm buildings beyond. The grass would actually have been 'enjoyed' by cattle belonging to Smiths farm who were tethered on the track rather than by their owners!

Caswalls Farm

This was the part of what is now the Bank House site that already belonged to the Hampton Court estate in 1663 when it was leased to Henry Caswall of Wicton, gent, for 99 years on the lives of his daughters, Philippa and Celia Caswall and his grandson, Henry Parker. The messuage leased was described as being 'in the township of Bodenham' and had formerly been in occupation of John Hooper, gent, presumably he who had given Smiths farm to Susan Smith in 1642. Along with Caswalls farm was leased a messuage at the Moor (now called Upper Moor Court) and another messuage, (unidentified as yet). The lease was confirmed in 1665 and by that time Henry Caswall had moved from Wicton and was actually living at Caswalls farm with Philippa and his son Fitzwilliam while the other daughter, Celia, had married a John Cook and was living at the 'messuage at the Moor'.

When Henry Caswall died in 1667 his inventory gives an interesting list of rooms and his possessions within them:

chamber over the hall ...2 beds with furniture belonging to them, 3 chests, 1 table, 3 chairs

at the stairs head .... 1 bed and bolster with the coverings

chamber over the kitchen..............1 bed and 1 side cupboard

in the hall .... table board and frame, 3 chairs, 3 joyne stools, 1 pr.andirons and a steele

in the kitchen..... 3 brass kettles, 2 brass pots, 3 brass pans, 3 brass posnetts, 6 pewter dishes,
     1 table board, 1 small cupboard, 1 jack, 2 spits, 2 iron dripping pans,1 pr.andirons

in the cellar......5 hogsetts and 3 barrels

linen of all sorts, fire wood in the fould, one mault mill

barley, pease and pouse (pulse) in the whole 3 acres and 3 swine

The whole was worth £17 - 04 - 04.

In 1684 Philippa Cook came to live with Fitzwilliam and Celia at Caswalls Farm on the death of her husband. She survived both her brother and her sister and in 1707 gave up the lease of the property in exchange for an annuity of £26 after which she appears to have moved away from the village.

The new tenant was Francis Sawyer who came from an old Bodenham family and it seems likely that the brick front was put on the house in his time or that of his son since the fine brickwork, in the expensive Flemish bond, would show that they were going up in the world. Upper Moor Court and the unidentified house were still included in the lease.

Later information—Bank House

After 1710 both Smiths Farm and Caswalls Farm were owned by the Hampton Court estate but throughout the eighteenth century information about them is rather scanty. However it seems probable that it was Smiths Farm that disappeared and Caswalls Farm, with its cellar, that survived and came to be called Bank House.

More detailed information about Bank House becomes available once estate record keeping got well established under the Arkwrights. In 1820 John Wanklin was the tenant with 41 acres in the fields around but he rented other farms in the parish as well and it seems to have been Thomas Wright (see 39) who was living in the house. Later the house was said to be in two cottages and certainly at the time of the 1841 census a great many people seemed to be living there including Thomas Wright.

As for Smiths farm there is no more information after it was marked on the 1813 map. When it disappeared is not known but it was probably soon after that date as the Arkwright Building Records, which recorded the taking down of buildings as well as their repair, give no indication of its presence. The house may well have just collapsed.

By 1848 Bank House was also in bad condition and the estate planned a radical change in its status. The agent writing at that date said: 'These premises lying in a dilapidated state the outside walls of the house alone were allowed to remain. The interior was entirely rebuilt viz: new partitions, walls, chimneys, etc'. The 1848 buildings records give more details of the work as it progressed including the names of two men who spent several days 'laying paving in the cellar'—an interesting record because the present owners do not know of a cellar below the house! The restoration made the house suitable for a gentleman's residence but, as was the estate's practice, the land was taken from it and only the garden and orchard left. It probably acquired the name of Bank House after the reconstruction as it then ceased to be a farm house.

The first tenant of the refurbished house was the curate, the Rev J.K. Harrison. When he left the parish he was presented with a very handsome silver inkwell, still treasured by his great, great grandson, and a purse of gold. In 1901 the house was occupied by one of Mr J.H. Arkwright's daughters who had married Richard Chester Master but by 1909 Henry Downes was the tenant and in the 1923 sale of the estate he bought Bank House (see 45).

This concludes a brief account of the complicated history of this site but mention must be made of the intriguing find of a small stone head in the infill of a wall that was being altered in the 1990s. The British Museum identified the head (from a photograph) as either a crude seventeenth-century carving or else as Romano-British. Three other such heads have been recorded in the county and are all described as Celtic. One of these is built into Panksbridge near Much Cowarne over the River Loddon and it has been suggested that it indicates a former Celtic shrine or water cult associated with the waterway. It is probable that the Bank House little head has local provenance as various stone walls were taken down in the 1848 restoration and it may well have came from these. Romano-British burials have been found near Ashgrove Farm, just over the border of Bodenham parish, so it seems likely that this little head is the oldest carved stone in Bodenham.

(42) Pound Cottage / the Post office / Chapel and (43) Bridge Cottage / Chapel (A63 /II / 230 / 1-6)

These two houses are considered together because for a long time they were part of the same homestead. The deeds begin in 1655 when Richard Hall of the Middle Temple, London sold the property to the occupiers, Thomas and Mary Wright. Nothing is known of Richard Hall but the Wrights were very much a Bodenham family at the time. (The grandson of Thomas and Mary, Daniel Wright, bought the Penthouse (39) and the subsequent history of the family can be followed there.) A later member of the family, another Thomas, sold the property to Richard Dyer, a local farmer when it was described as: 'a messuage with barn called the chapel'.

Two points are of interest in this description, firstly the name and secondly that there was only one house on the site. The name Chapel was in use for all this lower part of the village at one time, notably in the 1841 and 1851 censuses, but its origin is obscure. The name could perhaps refer to an ancient chapel by the bridge, a possibility suggested by the finding of a supposedly Romano-British carved stone head at Bank House (41). Certainly there is no evidence of a non-conformist chapel here but there is some evidence that Ford chapel owned land here at one time.

After buying the property Dyer 'developed' it by making the barn into two cottages and then in 1829 he sold the whole to Richard Arkwright. Writing at that time the agent commented:

> If Dyer's cottages ... are worth leaving standing their gardens might come up to the main road where the rick yards are at present and a wall made near the road. The old Pound might also be removed from its present situation.

The rickyards must have belonged to the Weirhouse Farm (44) and it seems that the agent's suggestions were carried out except that the Pound was not moved. The agent's doubts about the soundness of the cottages seem to have been well founded for one, probably the original cottage, was replaced by a new one. This was probably Pound Cottage and stone foundations of its predecessor have been found just in front of it.

Bridge Cottage and Pound Cottage

The other two cottages, made out of the barn, were 'altered and repaired'. The gardens were enclosed as suggested by a stone wall which incorporated the Pound in one of them. They were sold as separate cottages at the 1924 sale.

Very sadly most of the Pound (79) was later taken down only the part incorporated in the wall by the road as a slight bulge remaining today. It had been an important part of Bodenham life for a long time and was frequently mentioned in the proceedings of the manorial court .

(44) The Weirhouse / The School / Warehouse Farm / Pound Farm

This large house standing beside Bodenham Bridge has had a complicated history and many name changes. It was one of the properties that was owned in the eighteenth century by the Marquis of Bath (Devereux) and was sold with all the other Devereux properties in Bodenham to the Earl of Essex (Conyngsby) in 1803 and then to Richard Arkwright with the rest of the Hampton Court estate in 1810. As a result any old deeds that may survive will be held in the Longleat archives. A brief search here found leases back to 1724 when the house was a farm tenanted by the Wright family (see 39) and was always referred to as 'farm late Adams' or 'the Pound farm'. The latter name refers to the village pound (79) which stood nearby as its remains still do today.

The name 'late Adams' gives a clue to an earlier owner or tenant, possibly a Charles Adams who was one of the three signatories to the deed that set up the Conyngsby Hospital in Hereford c.1614, the other two being Sir Thomas Conyngsby himself and the then Vicar of Bodenham who was the first chaplain of the Hospital. The vicars of Bodenham were chaplains of the hospital for many years thereafter.

Other members of the Adams family lived in the village after Charles and since they were clearly gentry it seems probable that it was one of them who put the fine brick front, said to be mid eighteenth century, onto the existing timber-framed building.

By 1796 Joseph South was the tenant and in the vestry book he was referred to as 'of the Warehouse', the first use of that name that has been found. The Warehouse building itself is shown on the 1820 Enclosure map and was a long building running north-south, larger than the house itself and standing just to the south of it.. It seems possible that it could have been built as a warehouse to do with the navigation of the River Lugg, set up around 1700 but this was never very successful and by Joseph South's time the building was being used as 'an extensive malting'.

In 1803 the property was sold, along with all the Devereux property in Bodenham, to the Earl of Essex (Coningsby) and so became a part of the Hampton Court estate and at this time the malthouse and farm buildings were occupied by William Nicolls of Bank House (41) but the house was occupied by Rev John Taylor DD, perpetual curate of Ford who later went to Hope parish.

In 1810 the property came into the ownership of Richard Arkwright and various tenants followed including Charles Dunn, surgeon, who was appointed at a public meeting to attend the poor of the parish and 'inoculate for the cow pock, gratis'. He was paid £15 p.a. and 7s for each midwifery case. After him came another doctor, Henry Rudge and then a confusing succession of tenants occupying the land or the house or both. The writer of the report on the estate in 1828 found the situation very unsatisfactory and said:

> the house is too good for a common farmhouse and is now put with a small quantity of land (37 acres) to suit an amateur farmer on a small scale. The unsightly warehouse should come down and if the cottages [42 and 43] could be bought the whole rickyard area could be turned into a garden for them with a wall next the road. The pound should be moved.

His instructions were carried out except that the pound remained. The warehouse came down in 1830 after which a lot of men were employed in 'levelling the ground and building an embankment'.

The first amateur gentleman farmer to occupy the newly refurbished house was William Turberville, son of Matthew Turberville (see 23). He had three children born there and then moved to a larger farm at Orleton, clearly he had not been given enough land. But the original land was not returned to the house, instead, in 1840, the house was converted into a school and the land was split up and let to four existing estate tenants.

The school, under its master Edward Mason moved from Devereux Court (20) into the house. In 1845 James Morton came as head master with his wife Jane, who was schoolmistress, and twin sons. The school stayed in the house until 1863 when the Mortons moved their pupils into the purpose built new school (12).

The house was then converted into two cottages though this seems to have entailed very little in the way of alterations. It remained as two separate houses even after the 1923 sale when it was bought by Mr James Simpson, the organist who lived in one of the houses and sold the other. It continued thus in divided ownership until 1980 when it was made it into one house again.

The name 'Weirhouse' requires some explanation. The name 'Warehouse', taken from the old warehouse that stood on the site, was in regular use up to the Second World War though the building itself had long gone, but later occupants clearly thought the name too industrial and downmarket and so upgraded it to the 'Weirhouse'. In so doing an important part of the history of the house was lost and confusion was added for there is no evidence that there ever was a 'weir' on this stretch of the river!

(45) 'The Old Forge' / The Smithy / Sindale (E41 / 1)

The earliest known owner of this property was called Brace but by 1794 it was owned by one Benjamin Bowring who sold it in 1804 to the Hampton Court estate. At that time it was occupied by John Went, the first of three generations of that name, all blacksmiths, to occupy the smithy. There are earlier records of this family in the parish, a Henry Went, smith, at Marsh Maund in 1717 and another John Went, smith, in 1733 in the Moor.

When Richard Arkwright bought the Hampton Court estate in 1810 the smithy was described as: 'a well accustomed smith's shop and dwelling house with garden and orchard one acre'.

The house in which the Went family lived beside the smithy was called Sindale and is partly visible in a photo taken around 1900 of the bridge. The house stood parallel to the river, timber-framed with a roof of stone tiles and outbuilt chimney at the north gable. Parts of this house were later incorporated into the smithy buildings. As well as being a smithy it was evidently a small farm as it had a cow house, stable and calves cot.

Repairs carried out on the house after 1810 included 'plastering the walls and tarring the timbers' which seems to imply that before this the timbers were untreated oak. This indicates that in the eighteenth century and before Bodenham's timber-frame buildings were probably all brown and white—blackening being a later fashion. At the same time a stone wall was built 'beside the road'. This is presumably the wall, still present, which bounds the right of way leading from the road down to the river beside the bridge. There was also mention at this time of 'altering the penthouse'. According to Mr Trevor Barrar, who had worked at the smithy all his life, this was an open shed or part of the smithy where horses were tethered while being shod. Penthouse was also the earlier name for the Old Vicarage (39) and this too had been occupied by a smith.

By 1828 John Went had been joined by his son and when he died John Went junior employed Henry Wharton who lived over the road at Bridge Cottages (43). Then about 1860 the Went family moved across the road to Bank House (41) and it seems likely that Sindale was no longer inhabited after that. John Went the second died around 1880 and his widow carried on the business with her son, the third John Went, but the business no longer prospered and c.1905 the Arkwrights asked Henry Downes who worked on the estate to take it over.

At some time before 1923 the estate built a 'modern, brick built and tiled smith's shop and shoeing forge' to replace the old building. The grey slate roof of the forge had and still has distinctive finials at the two ends.

The Downes family lived first at Bank House and then at Lindale, a house built in the Bank House garden and named, in part, after the old smithy house. Three generations

The Forge

44

of the Downes family carried on the business until 1995 when the smithy was sold and converted into a house. For 170 years or more the smithy had been run by only two families, a remarkable story of continuity that has sadly now come to an end but many iron gates, examples of the fine craftsmanship from the smithy, can still be seen in gardens in the village and in the churchyard.

(46 - 51) Houses in the Dinmore part of the parish (B76/Box 14(33), A63/II / 237)

Before the coming of the railway this must have been a rather isolated area on the edge of Bodenham parish lying close under Dinmore Hill. The normal way to the church and village would have been along the 'West Lane' which ran along the bottom of the valley passing Lady Close (21) before coming into the village at the Cross Well. But when the floods were out the inhabitants would probably have had to climb the hill and go by the Henhouse(53) because the present road along the side of the hill was not made as a through route till 1813 (see 83).

At the start of the nineteenth century there seem to have been only three houses, **Rose cottage** (50), **Trilloes cottage** (51) and **Witchall** (46) present here of which only the first named still survives today. The most important of the three, a small farm, was called Witchall which was also the name for the whole area. An alternative spelling was 'Whitewall' which may give a clue to the origin of the name because there is a large tufa spring on the hill above and if there were no tree cover and the tufa were being actively quarried there would have been a white scar or 'wall' on the hillside (see Hill House (54) for more information on tufa).

The property that went by the name of Witchall was bequeathed in 1796 by Thomas Taylor, 'gent.'of Canon Pyon to John and Elizabeth Atkins, children of Thomas Atkins who had probably been a servant to Thomas Taylor. John Atkins was an agricultural labourer and under his ownership the house, which had a hop kiln and buildings, was mortgaged several times and doubtless was not properly maintained.

When John died in 1837 his mortgagee let the house to William Hall (see 32) who started to retail cider from the premises. By 1859 the Lingen family had become the owners and tried to sell the property to Mr Arkwright but he said he would only take it with vacant possession. So the Lingens sent 'a person to take possession but as the Halls were not provided with another house they had permission to remain nine days longer'. On the next attempt to move them the Halls had to stay 'to get up their potatoes' and so it went on. In the end Mr Arkwright bought the house with the Halls and their two lodgers, a railway porter and a telegraph clerk, still in residence. The estate re-thatched the house but only got vacant possession in 1872 when William Hall died. By that time the house had deteriorated beyond repair. It only cost £1-17-1 to pull down and the 'wood' was sold for £1. The house was probably timber-framed and it certainly had a thatched roof, but how old it was we cannot tell. There are only faint indications on the ground today to show where it stood.

Rose Cottage (50) still stands today. It was owned by Hampton Court and was improved and enlarged in the early nineteenth century to house first the estate shepherd and then a succession of gamekeepers. When it was sold in the 1923 sale it had 3 acres of land which probably included the site of **Trilloes cottage** (51). This too belonged to the estate but was said to be a 'miserable hovel' which was occupied in 1828 by an agricultural labourer called Trilloe and his large family but was later pulled down.

In 1852 land was sold to the Shrewsbury and Hereford Railway Co. and the eastern tunnel and bridge were built, the bricks supposedly coming from clay dug near the river. To ensure correct alignment of the tunnel a **Sighting Tower** was built on the hill above, the remains of which still stand. The **Station** (48) and **Railway cottages** (49) were also built at this time and Mr Arkwright also built an 'ornamental double cottage' called **Dinmore Cottage** (47). By 1855 this had become a public house and has remained as such ever since though the name has changed. It was known grandly as the 'Bellevue Hotel' at one time.

When the idea of the station was first mooted it was referred to as 'Witchill station' and it is a pity that it did not retain that name since not only would there be no confusion with Hope-under-Dinmore but we would know how the name Witchall was really pronounced.

The second tunnel was built in 1891 and at that time the church built a Reading Room in the woods nearby for the tunnel workmen and held services there on Sundays.

The Railway Inn   *The Sighting Tower*

(52) Hollybush Cottage / Wagnells (A63 / 1 / 61 & 81)

This cottage, which had gone by the 1980s, stood on the top of Dinmore Hill to the west of the Henhouse (53) (it had nothing to do with the lane to Pencombe which is today called Hollybush Lane).

The cottage belonged to the Hampton Court estate from at least 1680 when it was described as: 'Cottage and one acre and a parcel of land lately enclosed out of land called the Lyes and half an acre lying by the side of the lane leading from Bodenham to Howe Wood'. Howe Wood was a part of the Dinmore Hill woodland and the document quoted from above was a lease from Thomas Coningsby of Hampton Court to John Harris. The Harris family were still tenants in 1810 but had sub-let to Joseph Bolton whose 'kneeling' in the church was described as for 'Bolton for a tenement near the Henhouse'. At that time the cottage still had four acres of land. Soon after it was tenanted by someone called Wagnall and he was probably the last person to occupy it. By this time the area had become covered by trees, probably the wood which today is called 'Hollybush plantation'.

On the 1887 map the house was not marked but where it had been shown on earlier maps Mr Jack Weyman Jones said there had been the remains of a building and a Damoscene tree, a cross between a Damson and a Plum. In the 1980s there were Currant bushes in the same area and a large Walnut tree, fallen but still very much alive, with several large, upstanding branches making a row of young Walnut trees.

It is probable that in earlier times there was another cottage nearby for a rental of 1716 describes a 'cottage, garden and two acres near the How Wood Gate' occupied by Thomas Colcombe and then later by John Lane.

(53) The Henhouse and a cottage that stood near it (A63 / III / 14)

According to the map the Henhouse itself is not quite in Bodenham parish though there is a story current that the inhabitants cook their meals in Hope parish and eat them in Bodenham—in other words that the parish boundary runs through the house. The house is isolated today but earlier days there were at least four dwellings in the area, the Henhouse itself, two cottages described under the Hollybush (52) and another cottage which was recorded in 1821 as being 'taken down' whose former position is uncertain and the settlement was situated on one of the two main east west routes through Bodenham (see 83).

The Henhouse site may well be a very old one since Dr Stanford places it within the ramparts of a very large iron age fort and the name 'hen' may come from the Welsh for 'old'.

In 1789 one of the fields going with the Henhouse at that time was called 'Old Parkes', a name which may indicate an earlier deer park for Hampton Court, later replaced by the deer park on the other side of the main road. If this were indeed so then the Henhouse might have started life as a park keepers lodge.

The Henhouse farm was a part of the estate when Richard Arkwright bought it. In 1769 it had been leased to John Monk (see 63) and consisted of a 'dwelling house, barn, stable, beast house and 74 acres'. At the time of the 1810 sale it was described as 'messuage and farm buildings with 181 acres' and was occupied by a widow, Ann Vale, and her son William who were soon replaced as tenants by George Webb. The house had evidently got into a bad state and the building records at that time indicate that a lot of work was done on it: 'the greatest part of the house new and a general repair of the out-buildings £346'. But, as was typical of the estate, the house was not pulled down and rebuilt from scratch and older parts remained. The original house was fairly certainly timber-framed for the western gable still remains together with one bay at the west end and the stone out-built chimney and there are indications that the timber framing once extended further east. All the eastern part of the house probably dates from the rebuilding quoted above and is of stone, but stone of a different type to that used in the west chimney. The house was probably tiled when it was rebuilt but the stable and cowhouse were thatched at that time. After the rebuilding the farm was run with Hampton Green farm but was said to be 'inconvenient on account of the distance from that farm and the height'.

It was occupied by first the farm bailiff, William Sessions (see 70) and then D.J. Thomas, clerk of the works. But by 1905 it was being farmed from the other side of the hill with Bodenham Court Farm (31) by Richard Medlicott. Later when Lord and Lady Hereford bought the estate it was being farmed by an old man called Michael who paid no rent and made what money he could from rabbits and blackberries, the farm being so overgrown—one field was said to be white with sheep bones. When Mr Jack Weyman Jones became tenant of Bodenham Court Farm Lady Hereford made it one condition of the tenancy that he took on the Henhouse as well, and so he installed his own shepherd in the house.

Subsequently there was a bad fire, the inside of the house was gutted and the roof destroyed. The house remained uninhabitable until 1978 when the then owner of the estate had it thoroughly repaired by a Leominster builder. New stairs were put in and the roof raised at the back to make a very attractive house which was then occupied by the estate gamekeeper and his family.

(54) Hill House / The Hill / The Weaving Shed

This is one of the very few properties in the Township that never belonged to the Arkwrights though they rented it for a period on one occasion.

From the eighteenth century until 1941 it belonged first to the Bucklee family and then to their descendants the Landons. Four generations of Bucklees (or Bucknells), all called Thomas, lived here and in their time up to about 1830 the house was called the Hill. This name was distinct from that of Bodenham Hall (23) which up to 1820 was called Hill House. The Bucklees were evidentially fairly prosperous yeomen farmers owning a fair amount of land. At least two of them were weavers as well and left 'looms and other instruments of their trade' to their descendants but oddly enough the name 'Weaving shed' for the building just to the west of the house dates from a quite different weaver who occupied the house at a later date.

The house is situated on a steep south facing slope and until 1813 was approached from the village by the old West Lane running along the valley below (see section on roads). When the first house was built we do not know. A Thomas Bucknell owned a small field here in 1707 but there is no mention of a house. The third Thomas Bucklee died in 1822 and the ownership of the property passed to his son Thomas Bucklee (IV) but he sold it to his sister Mary and her husband Richard Landon and it remained with the Landon family for four generations. In 1851 it was occupied by Thomas Landon who was described as an 'army clothier'. He was also the Surveyor for the area and the man who gave permission for the erection of the upright stone which stands in the socket of the old market cross on the village green (see 81).

By 1858 the Landons had let the house to Mr Arkwright for 21 years with 13 acres and the estate carried out a lot of refurbishment to prepare the house for occupancy by Col. Chester-Master and his wife, one of Mr Arkwright's daughters.

Various tenants followed the Chester-Masters including Henry Ashworth, agent for the estate, around 1900. His widow said that she had been told of the use of the road along the bottom of the valley as the main approach to the house. Later the house was occupied by Captain Appleton who started a hand-weaving business in the building just to the west of the house. This was known as the Weaving Shed and later on was converted into a house. Girls came to work in the business by train and the bungalow above the road was built for a woman who washed all the woven cloths. It is an odd coincidence that the property should twice have been occupied by weavers, though at very different dates.

In 1941 Rev H.R. Landon bequeathed the property to Worcester College, Oxford who later sold the house and the land.

Just to the west of Hill House and the Weaving Shed is a track that formerly led down to a ford over the River Lugg to the Vern and slightly further west 'the waterfall' flows down just above the road and continues below it. This water comes from a petrifying spring in the wood just above. Over the years this spring has deposited large amounts of tufa on the hillside in this area which is called 'Hoarstone Rough' both above and below the road. There was so much tufa that in 1702 the Hampton Court estate granted a lease to quarry 'rock of limestone or hoarstone' here with a right of way for its removal, presumably by horse and cart. Fragments of tufa have been found in the soil of the field below radiating out from the base of the waterfall across the flood plain nearly as far as the river so it was probably a very large deposit and is one possible site for the tufa in Bodenham church walls. Trial borings made before building a new drive to the Weaving Shed produced a great depth of 'white stuff' which was probably also tufa. In the late nineteenth or early twentieth century water from the spring was piped along the hillside to the Ladywell (82) to augment the water supply in the village.

(55) Bodenham Manor / The Vicarage

This house was built in 1844 as a new Vicarage for the parish. It was built to house Bodenham's new vicar, the Rev Henry Arkwright who was a nephew of John Arkwright of Hampton Court.

The earlier vicarage (13) had been out of use for some years and, even if not too dilapidated, would have been far too small for Bodenham's grand new vicar. While the new vicarage was being built Henry Arkwright and his family lived at the Penthouse (39).

Before the new vicarage could be built two legal matters had to be settled. Firstly, because the chosen site lay right across the main road west out of the village, this had to be replaced and the stretch of road which today runs from the bottom of Ladywell Lane up to the gate of Bodenham Manor was built new at this time.

Secondly there had to be a legal exchange of land between the church and the Hampton Court estate by which the old vicarage (13) and its land came to the estate and the new vicarage and its lands came into church ownership.

When these matters were settled a new quarry was opened up nearby and work on the house started. The building was all done by the estate workforce and Henry Arkwright moved in in 1850 with his second wife, seven children and a large establishment consisting of governess, butler, housekeeper and seven servants. He was to stay there until his death in 1889.

The vicar who followed him, Rev H.C. Sturges, could not possibly afford to live in such a large house and so, after another glebe exchange, he took up residence at the Penthouse (39) and Henry Arkwright's vicarage reverted to the Hampton Court estate again. There was a suggestion that it should be called 'Westfield Manor', a name derived from the former open arable field on which the house was built but sadly the misleading name of 'Bodenham Manor' was adopted instead. The house was let, first to Mr and Lady King-King and then to the Starey family.

After the sale of the Hampton Court estate the house was occupied for a time by 'some sort of women in floating robes given to falling into trances in the woods' according to one former resident, and a small boy from one of the Ladywell Lane cottages (25) going with his mother to pay the rent was frightened of going to the house because of the 'monks', as he remembered in later life.

(56 & 57) The Vern and the old Vern

The Vern is very much on the boundary between Bodenham and Marden and from medieval times onwards the two settlements shared some of their open arable fields including Ashgrove field. This resulted in the extraordinary interlocking boundary between the two parishes shown on the enclosure map of 1813 where some strips in one of the parishes are even entirely surrounded by land in the other parish.

At the time of Domesday the Vern was a separate manor from Bodenham Devereux under a different lord and its ownership has always been different. But at the time of the Inclosure map in 1813 the Vern was included in the Township of Bodenham Devereux and as a result a brief account of it is included here.

The name Vern or Fern does not just apply to the one house that carries the name today but to the whole area. It has been postulated that in medieval times there was a whole village here.

There are certain key dates when some sort of estimate of the population of the area is given

1662   Militia assessment—seven men named, the most prosperous being William Towne

1665   Hearth Tax—eight houses taxed

1801   Census—sixteen inhabited houses

1813 and 1914 Enclosure map and Vern Tithe map—on both these maps two main groups of buildings are shown, one around the present Vern house and the other to the south-west called 'old homestead' or 'old Vern'.

Up to the twentieth century the Vern always had an absentee landlord. It was granted by the Crown to John Scudamore of Holme Lacy in 1687 and from him descended to the Duke of Norfolk and his heirs who finally sold it in 1909 to Richard Medlicot (see 31).

The tenants seem always to have centred their activities on Bodenham rather than Marden and their memorials are in Bodenham church. William Towne died in 1667 and his inventory shows he was a wealthy farmer. His house consisted of 'Hall, Parlour, chamber over the parlour, chamber at the stairhead, buttery with chamber over, kitchen and dairy'. He had 6 oxen, 8 kine, 3 mares and a colt, swine, sheep and extensive crops.

He was followed by Thomas and Richard Evans and then John and Thomas Mason, Thomas Bennet, Lot Newman (see 21), Thomas Burlton and William Price (see 23).

After the estate was sold both Richard Medlicot and Captain de Quincey who followed him were notable breeders of Hereford cattle. Captain de Quincey established the gardens and was said to have imported a whole trainload of peat via Dinmore station so that he could grow Rhododendrons in Bodenham's alkaline soils. He was also the first person to breed Humming birds in this country—they nested apparently in the bathroom. Mrs de Quincey founded and was Captain of Bodenham's first Guide company which is remembered as a very active and happy group (see 26).

Communication with Bodenham village was probably easier then than with Marden and more direct. There must always have been some sort of crossing of the River Lugg beside the church but there was also long-established ford near the house which was repaired in 1672. The track from this would have joined the West Lane leading to the village. Later there was a private footbridge over the river whose use was restricted to residents of the Vern. This was swept away by floods in 1924 together with a cow. The latter was rescued from a long way down stream and returned home unharmed but the bridge was never replaced. Its footings on the right bank were still visible in the 1980s till removed by gravel workings.

As for the area known as 'old vern' very little has been found. In the early nineteenth century it was often mentioned under the name of 'Sargents Farm' and in 1805 the Duke of Norfolk paid for a kneeling in Bodenham church for 'Elizabeth Sargants farm at the Vern'. In 1814 four buildings were marked here but probably only one was a house. Then in 1818 Lot Newman was tenant of 'late Mrs Sargants' so it seems that by then it had been incorporated into the Vern.

(57b) Orchard Cottage / Vern Cottage

This cottage, built in the late seventeenth century was occupied by John Bradley of Fern in 1702 and there were still Bradleys there in 1813. By the 1930s it was owned by Captain de Quincey and occupied by the Middleton family. Other cottages in this area are in Marden Parish.

(58) The Bunhill Barn / one of the two Tithe Barns

The early history of the two timber-framed Tithe barns that stood to the east of Bodenham church has been described under (2). Both barns were moved in the early nineteenth century, one to Bodenham Court Farm (31) but the other out into what was the former open field known as Bunhill Field. It stands beside the track going up between the Old Vicarage (39) and Bank House (41).

There is no evidence that there was ever an earlier settlement or house in this place but it was common practice in the eighteenth and nineteenth centuries, when the old open arable fields were being enclosed and divided up, to erect out-buildings to service the new, smaller fields. These buildings usually consisted of a barn to store the hay or corn and a fold-yard to shelter the cattle. On most estates these buildings would have been built new but it was in keeping with the Arkwrights' methods of estate management at that time to re-use old buildings wherever possible and so a new use was found for the old Tithe barn.

The estate repaired the barn and cattle sheds in 1828 and several times after that but oddly enough there is no record of any work being done in 1871 though that date is carved on one of the struts of the central truss.

(59, 60, 60A & 61) Cottages in Ketch Lane & Millcroft Lane area

This flat low-lying area between Bodenham, Englands Gate and Saffrons Cross floods very badly when the three streams that cross the area, Riffins Brook, the Moor Brook and Millcroft Brook (formerly called Grit Pit Brook) overflow their banks. Never-the-less in the nineteenth century four cottages stood here all of which are long gone leaving few traces of their existence.

(59) Storehouse / Ketch Lane Cottage / Watery Lane Cottage/ Ketch Gate

This cottage survived the longest of the four and its garden was only incorporated into the field next door in the 1990s. The differently coloured garden soil is still distinguishable from that of the field when it is all ploughed.

The land on which the cottage was built was described in 1713 as 'a parcel of meadow called Millcroft Gate', a name which indicates that the gate into the large open arable field called Millcroft was nearby. At this time the land was being given by Thomas Baker to his brother Philip, along with Englands Gate (64) with which property it descended to John Gillum who probably built the cottage and then sold both inn and cottage to the Hampton Court estate.

The house seems originally to have been occupied as a 'double cottage' by two families, despite having only one chimney and one oven which both families used. In 1828 the agent had more land added to the cottage as he felt there was not enough garden to feed two families. It was described then as a: 'stone and grey slate cottage with porch, 4 rooms, back kitchen and offices'.

Later the cottage went with Bodenham Court Farm (31) and Mr Jack Weyman-Jones remembered taking food to the family living there on horseback at times of flood. Drinking water came from a tap across the bridge by Bank House (41) though later a stand pipe was put up in the lane nearby. The house was pulled down in the 1960s and two loads of stone were taken up to Tan-y-Bryn (17), to build a rock garden, but the land remained with the estate, fenced off from the rest of the field, until the 1990s.

Ketch Lane Cottage

(60) Cottage on Millcroft / Watery Lane

This was a short-lived cottage built, according to map evidence, between 1813 and 1828 though the land it was built on was enclosed out of Millcroft Field at an earlier date. The cottage was probably occupied in 1841 by Thomas Daw who was a schoolmaster. His son too was called Thomas and writing a hundred years later the vicar said: 'about 1800 a school was kept by Thomas Daw's father opposite the Millcroft (62) where formerly three houses stood. In times of flood people had to be carried out in boats'.

From around 1846–1871 the cottage was occupied by Thomas Penson, an agricultural labourer. It was originally thatched but later had its roof tiled. By 1887 the cottage had gone, the only sign of its former presence being a gooseberry bush in the roadside hedge. This always comes into leaf earlier than the other bushes beside it.

(60A) Ketch Cottage / The Octagon Cottage

This cottage does not actually appear on any map but, in a report for the Hampton Court estate, the surveyor suggested building an 'octagon cottage on a small scale' at the junction of Ketch and

Millcroft Lanes, quite a conspicuous spot. He drew a ground plan and sketch of the proposed cottage which he said would cost £18 to build and it seems that the cottage was actually built for in 1832 the Building Records note: 'Ketch cottage, tenant William Bowcott, a new cottage and levelling the ground and enclosing the garden'.

The materials used were lathe, stone, timber, hair etc which suggests a timber-framed cottage on a stone base. In 1835 a privy was added. The cottage was probably occupied by Mary Hynam, then Martha Henwood and then James Taylor.

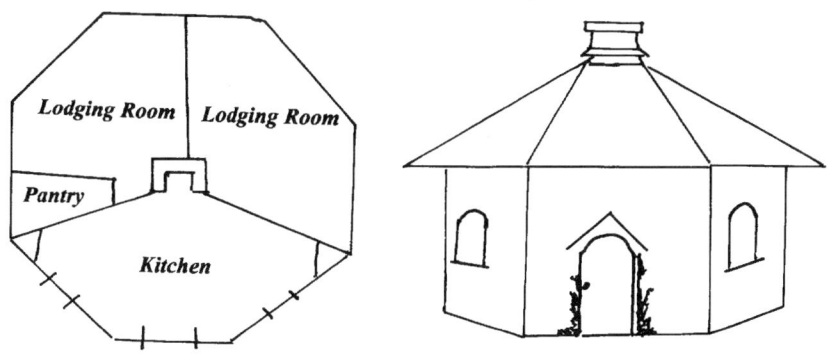

Ground plan and elevation of The Octagon Cottage

Octagon cottages were quite the thing at that period among large landowners and one can imagine the women folk of the family gathering to curtsey at the door of the cottage as the Arkwright coach went by, thus adding to the picturesque attraction of the cottage to its owner.

(61) Watery Lane Cottage / Shepherd's Cottage on Millcroft (B76 / Box 4)

This cottage stood on slightly higher ground than the previous three and was older than any of them. On the 1813 map it is marked as an L-shaped building just opposite Millcroft Farm (62). In the title deeds it was described before 1738 as: 'cottage where Anne Symonds lived, enclosed out of Millcroft Field'. Anne was the widow of Philip Symonds to whom it had formerly belonged. The cottage was subsequently sold or bequeathed to Thomas Fowler and then John Newton followed by Susan Hill and her two sons John and Thomas who sold it to Richard Arkwright in 1828.

A report in 1828 on the estate properties says of this cottage: 'Shepherds cottage, late Hills, wants some fencing in front and some walls plastering and pig styes removed'. The cottage was probably timber-framed and was certainly thatched. After 1828 it became a double cottage housing two families but apparently without any alterations being made so that two families had to share the fire and other facilities as seems to have been normal at this time.

Under the Arkwrights a succession of tenants followed: Joseph Shepherd, Henry Merrick, Thomas Beales and John Mytton in one of the cottages and William Mason, William Bethel and James Bullock in the other.

The cottage was re-thatched many times, the last being in 1870, but by 1887 it had gone and the land it stood on had become a part of Millcroft Field again, gooseberry bushes in the hedge are today the only indication of its former presence.

(62) Millcroft

This timber-framed, thatched house was built between 1657 and 1708 on two acres of arable land 'newly enclosed out of Elm Field'. Elm Field was one of Bodenham's medieval, open arable fields and extended from Millcroft Lane southwards. Oddly enough however the house took its name from another open arable field, Millcroft Field, lying on the other side of the lane. This field in turn took its name presumably from the water mill (81) that formerly stood on the River Lugg nearby. The house was probably built by Thomas Hodges who was a carpenter and it was owned by the Hodges family until 1776 when they sold it to John Monk (see 63) complete with: 'cider mill with runner, cheese vat. press, crooks, sill windlass. levers and appurtenances to the said cider mill belonging'.

John Monk lived there until his death in 1815. He left the property to his relatives, Thomas and Hannah Harris, but it was encumbered with paying the interest on £100 to Ann Gladding (see 8), a niece of John Monk's. The yearly interest Thomas Harris could manage but on Ann Gladding's death he had to pay out the capital of £100 to her family which was too much and forced him to sell Millcroft to the Hampton Court estate. As always the estate allowed Thomas and his wife to remain in the house for their lives. The roof was thatched and they were also given a small annuity.

When they died a lot of work was done on the property which included altering the course of the brook and building a new bridge with the stable on top of it and repairing the 'house, wain-house, stable, shed. calves cot and goose cots'. Then in 1911 the estate sold the farm to William Pritchard Williams of Brockington Farm (63).

(63) Brockington / Brockington Farm / Upper Brockington / Brockhampton (C69 /20)

This farmhouse, which was taken down c.1969 to make way for the new housing estate, was the largest and most important of the old buildings that have gone in Bodenham in recent years and there seems no good reason why the house itself should not have been spared. The name Brockington means 'brook dwellers settlement' which certainly fits the situation of the house, close to the stream which comes down from Dudales Hope.

Luckily the house was included in the 1931 RCHM survey which has left us with a photo of the house and a ground plan The surveyor said that the timber-frame house had been built in the early eighteenth century. Unfortunately Brockington never belonged to the Hampton Court estate and the title deeds have not been seen. The house may have been built by the Newton family, quite likely on the site of an earlier house for a James Newton held two houses in 'Brockhampton' around 1620 and a burial of 'Humphrey Newton of Brockington' was recorded in 1710. By 1777 it was probably owned by John Monk and then by 1800 by James Pitt who sold it to Thomas Symonds of Stoke Prior.

Then in 1837 it was for sale again when it was put up for auction with The Village (37) and Bunhill Villa (40) and described as:

> two kitchens, back kitchen, sitting room, large parlour, brewhouse, dairy, five good bedrooms, barn, cowhouse, stable, cider mill, hop kiln, granary, two good cellars, a pump of water, stream through the fold, 8 pieces of rich meadow, pasture, arable and hop land, 10 acres planted with the choisest apple and pear trees in the county and now in full bearing capable of producing 100 hogsheads a year, 17acres.

The Arkwrights were sufficiently interested to get the sale catalogue from which the above description is taken but sadly did not buy the property. Instead it came into the hands of the

Pritchard Williams family and after them of brother and sister Wilfred and Marjorie Medlicot (see 31). They later built a large house on the Ledbury road and called it Brockington Hall after their old home.

Since the Siward James Close was built on some of the Brockington land this is a suitable place to record something about the benefactor whose name is commemorated here. Mr Siward James was born in Birmingham in 1873 and

Brockington Farm

spent his working life as a solicitor there being one of Birmingham's prominent citizens for over 50 years. But his family came from Leominster where his uncles had been mayor on many occasions and he loved Herefordshire. He had no children but wished that his James ancestors should be remembered in the area. His nearest relative was his cousin and godson Kenneth V. James Moore who farmed Houghton Court. Tom James Moore, son of Kenneth, was one of the executors of Siward's will, in which he left money to build old people's homes in memory of his family. As a result land in Bodenham was bought, the houses were built on it and the whole was named after Siward James (the name Siward should be pronounced with a long 'i' as in fine).

(64) Englands Gate / Inlands Gate (B76 / Box 4)

The name of this property is unusual and derives from the name of one of Bodenham's ancient, open, arable fields. The name 'Englands Field' seems to be a corruption of the earlier name, 'Inland Field', which may refer to a period before the medieval open fields when the land belonging to a settlement was divided simply into an 'infield', near the settlement which was intensively cultivated, and the 'outfield' which was all the rest. The name 'Gate' probably refers to the farm gate that would have led into Englands Field. The manorial records have many references to the repair of such gates leading into the open fields.

The house is said to have been built in the seventeenth century and when Richard Arkwright bought the property in 1827 he acquired with it an extensive bundle of deeds. These start in 1665 when the property, described as 'Inlands gate', was owned by Thomas Baker. By 1713 it was owned by Philip Baker, described as 'servitor' who gave 'the messuage called Englands Gate situate at Englands Gate near a field called Englands Field' to his son, William. In 1713 both Philip and William Baker were described as 'corvisors' and in 1729 by the simpler term for the trade as 'shoemakers'.

There is an indication that the Bakers may already have been selling ale when in 1717 Philip is described as 'servitor' and certainly when William on his death was described as 'maltster'. Father and son were also farmers and were buying land in Bodenham's open fields: 3 acres in Berrington Field, 1 acre near Lugg Bridge, 1 acre in Dale Field, $1^{1}/_{2}$ acres in Inlands Field, 1 acre and 6 ridges in Millcroft Field, 5 acres in Bowley Meadow and land in Dunfield. The scattered nature of their holdings was typical of open field farming and the amount of land that they farmed indicates that at that time brewing and selling ale was only one of their activities.

William Baker was followed by a great nephew, John Gillum, who was the first member of the family to be actually called a 'victualler' but he does not seem to have been running a very successful business for by 1823 he was taking out a mortgage on the property and then in 1827 he sold it to the Hampton Court estate. The writer of a report in 1828 did not think very much of the estate's new acquisition:

> These premises want same convenient stabling and other outbuildings ... it is considered that the west side would be the best for the buildings - to build up to the height of the floor and after the old wood-framed building to come on the top and be boarded. ... The land let to this place is detached and scattered and when an opportunity offers so that it could be got nearer together detached pieces might be put to other places near. There should be 40 or 50 acres of land with the house to make the business worthwhile the attendance of a man for a woman alone could do little at a lone public house among unruly people.

It is probable that most of the recommendations were carried out and that the old building that was moved is the timber-framed building now standing to the south-west of the inn. The walls of this are said to be the same age as the house the roof being newer. This building was probably made into a malthouse in 1849 and pottery flues probably from this have been found but no malting tiles. Later a lot of old farm buildings, barn, stable, cowhouse, pig sties, cider mill and hop kiln were all pulled down as the premises ceased to be used as a farm as well as an inn. The house was originally thatched but stone slates replaced the thatch in 1855. A freak storm seems to have hit Bodenham in November 1852 when the tenant was allowed money to repair windows 'broken in a severe hail storm'.

In 1869 new windows were put into the large room over the

Englands Gate

stables which was then used as the club room for the friendly society known as Court Arkwright. For a short time around 1856 the landlord, Francis Green, added to his duties by becoming post master and an old photo of Englands Gate (reproduced in the Bodenham Old Photograph book) probably shows a group of people meeting the post outside the inn.

The estate sold Englands Gate to Frank Chilman in 1921 from whom it passed to Mr Shelley senior and then to his son.

(65) Humble Bee Hall (B76 / Box 14)
The delightful name of this cottage, which was certainly in use by 1727, was probably given by way of a joke because the building was so tiny. It stood opposite Englands Gate (64) as shown on a map and belonged to John and Sibble Newton in the early eighteenth century. Their descendants sold it in 1765 to Abraham Nutt, a labourer, for £13 - 8 - 0 when it was said to be not worth a mortgage 'for the said cottage is fallen down and greatly gone to decay'. Never-the-less Abraham Nutt lived there for over 50 years. After his death his grandson sold the cottage to John Gillum of Englands Gate and the Gillum family retained the cottage, after selling the inn to Hampton Court, and it was inherited by a nephew, James Norman who was a carter. He sold Humble Bee Hall to the estate but went on living there. The cottage was then re-thatched and the barn and pigsty repaired but after James Norman died the cottage was taken down in 1874.

Today cars, speeding along the new bit of the main road that bypasses Englands Gate, drive over the site of this little thatched cottage which once stood at the cross roads there with its farm buildings and ancient perry pear trees.

(66) Eastnor Castle (B76 / Box 14)
This cottage stood on the right of Woodhouse Lane between 'Evendine' and the Police House. Its grand name, like that of Humble Bee Hall (65), was given because of its small size. It was not marked on the 1813 map but by 1841 James Newman, an agricultural labourer, his wife and two children were living there.

It was sold by the Newman family to the Hampton Court estate in 1848 but James continued to live there for the rest of his life. The cottage was re-thatched once or twice and at the time of the 1923 estate sale was described as: 'a stucco and thatched cottage with two good orchards, 4 rooms with out offices'. But soon after it was gone, a Mrs Stephens being the last person to live there.

(67) Cottage at Calderwell (A 63 / III)
This cottage stood in Millcroft Field opposite Calderwell Farm (70) on the other side of the road.

It stood near to the 'Caldo Well', a spring said to have never run dry and providing especially cold, refreshing water. In 1694 a stream ran from this spring down to Riffins Brook.

The cottage was a part of the Hampton Court estate when Richard Arkwright bought it and may well have been the 'cottage with two gardens at Caldoe well' that was leased to Walter Herring in 1687.

In 1821 the estate repaired the walls, floor and oven and leased the cottage to the overseers of Hope parish, presumably to house their paupers, but later, after re-thatching, it was let to James

Hall. Then in 1836 this cottage was 'given in exchange to Daniel Wright for a cottage in Bodenham' (10A) and he was still living there in 1851 aged 80. Who came after him is not known but around 1880 the cottage ceased to be inhabited and disappeared though remains of its former presence were still visible in the 1970s.

Old leases exist to other cottages in the area that are no longer present so clearly there was quite a settlement here in earlier times, probably based on the good spring of abundant water.

(68) Calderwell Cottage / Bowkers, Calderwell

This cottage was built in the early 18th century and is timber-framed under stucco. It was thatched until 1856 at which date it was 'tiled'. In 1813 it was owned and occupied by John Bowker who, in his will of 1821, left it to his two sons, William and John, with the unusual and considerate proviso that: 'The two corner cupboards are to remain in my present dwelling as heirlooms for the use and benefit of the persons who may be entitled to my dwelling house'. (Much later Mr Poole, who owned the cottage for a short time, said the cupboards were no longer there though oddly enough there was a very old, built-in cupboard at Calderwell Farm (70) itself.)

In 1831 the cottage was subdivided, as so often happened, with William Bowker living in a part and his daughter with her husband living in 'the parlour and room over it and garden belonging to it'. In 1849 William sold the house to Hampton Court with the condition that he and his wife were to continue to live in their part of the house until their deaths.

There was a barn in the angle between the main road and Woodhouse Lane which was thatched at first but later 'tiled'. This was probably the building described as 'tiled cider and press house' in the 1923 estate sale catalogue.

(69) Cottage beside Calderwell Farm

This was another of Bodenham's ephemeral cottages with a life of probably less than one hundred years. Around 1810 it was being rented by Charles Philips from the Hampton Court estate for £3 per annum. The estate re-thatched the roof at intervals and the Philips family, father and then son, were still tenants in 1877 when the estate sold the cottage to W.W. Sessions of Calderwell Farm (70).

It stood just west of this farmhouse, end on to the road with a chimney at the north end. A long-time inhabitant of Bodenham remembered the cottage being inhabited by a rather flighty wife who was always swinging on the garden gate beside the road when her husband came home from work at 'Hampton' with the other waggoners instead of having a meal ready for him as a good wife should. The stone posts of the garden gate are still present in the hedge and the ground where the cottage stood is very uneven. Between this ground and Calderwell Farm is a high retaining wall made of stone which may well have come from the cottage. When or why the house was allowed to fall down is not known

(70) Calderwell Farm / Caldoe Well

In 1676 a farm called Caldoe Well was rented to a John Simons by Humphrey Conyngsby of Hampton Court as recorded in a rent roll of that date. This could well have been Calderwell. In

1709 Humphrey Newton was the tenant but throughout the nineteenth century the farm belonged to the Symonds family. This was a long-standing family in the parish. A Richard Symonds was churchwarden in 1662 when his name was inscribed on the beautiful chalice of that date and in 1740 Jonathan Symonds was one of the overseers for the parish. In 1805 a John Symonds occupied land in Millcroft Field (opposite Calderwell Farm) and in 1821 Jonathan Symonds was paying pew rent in the church for Calderwell. In 1841 John Symonds the elder was described as a 'yeoman' living at Calderwell and John Symonds the younger was described as a 'carpenter and inn keeper' at the Ketch (72).

By 1851 John Symonds the younger had moved to Calderwell Farm and was being described as a 'landed proprietor', the family were evidently moving up in the world. He and his wife indicated their higher status by giving their daughter two christian names—Olive Elizabeth—this was unusual among yeoman farmers at the time though common among the gentry.

Olive Elizabeth married William Washington Sessions, the farm bailiff for Hampton Court and in due course inherited Calderwell Farm. The Sessions bought more land in Millcroft Field and the cottage beside Calderwell Farm (69). But something seems to have gone wrong for they then mortgaged the farm, put in a tenant and moved up to Lancashire where W.W. Sessions became Head Gamekeeper to Lord Sefton at Croxteth Park. He had 22 keepers under him. As a result he was able to pay off the mortgage on Calderwell Farm. His son inherited the property but never lived there and sold to Percy Shuker, son of Langley Shuker, who subsequently sold it to Maurice Poole.

As for the buildings the barn is said to be early seventeenth century and part of the house may be the same age. But the wing with the brick front facing the road was built later and is not shown on the 1813 map. This fits well with the tradition that the bricks of which this wing was fronted formed the first load to cross the new bridge at Hampton Court, on their way from the estate brickworks to Calderwell. This bridge was erected by the Turnpike trustees around 1835.

(71) Yeoman's Ketch Lane Cottages (B 76 / Box 14)

This pair of semi-detached cottages stood on the west side of Ketch Lane and had a very short life—less than a hundred years. The cottages were built by Richard Yeoman of the New Inn (27) and since he was a stone-mason they were probably built of stone. They were built on land in Millcroft Field which Richard Yeoman had bought with the New Inn from his step-son. In 1861 two agricultural labourers were his tenants but in 1866 he sold the pair of cottages to the Hampton Court estate who made them into one. This involved a lot of repair work including making stairs.

At the same time most of the two acres of orchard that the estate had bought with the cottages was added to the adjacent farm land and a new' rail fence' put up and 'hedge of quicks' planted to enclose the cottage garden. Charles Shayle was the estate's first tenant but soon after the cottage was sold with other land around to William Washington Sessions of Calderwell Farm (69).

After this records cease. The cottage was still there in 1904 but it is not known when it was last inhabited or when taken down. Signs of foundations were still present in the ground in the 1980s and there are still snowdrops in the hedge marking the site.

(72) Saffrons Cross / Saffrons Cross Farm / Seavins Cross / The Ketch / The Catch

(B76 / Box 16)

This house was built in the seventeenth century but the title deeds do not begin until the nineteenth century. However a number of scattered references to the area have been found. In 1668 the place was called 'Sevan Cross' in the court rolls, in 1727 it was 'Savins Cross' and in 1754 it was marked as 'Seavons Cross' on Isaac Taylor's map of that date. The 1813 enclosure award refers to it as 'homestead called the Catch' and the lane that leads to the house from Bodenham bridge is called 'Ketch lane'.

In 1813 the property was owned by a Thomas Smith and occupied by Francis Green who was probably running it as a cider house and later moved to Englands Gate (64). He was followed by Jonathan Symonds (see 70) who was a carpenter as well as an innkeeper. After him came John Dykes, described as 'cider and beer retailer' who with his wife upgraded the place, in name at least, by calling it The George.

All this time the Smith family continued as the absentee owners but in 1885 Walter Foss Smith of London sold the property to the Hampton Court estate when it was described as: 'Saffrons Cross Farm situate at the Ketch, a messuage or public house, farm house, buildings and several closes, 16 acres'. The Arkwrights adapted the property to make it into Hunt Kennels and in 1889 it was recorded that: 'hounds were brought to the new kennels at the Ketch from the kennels at White Cross, Hereford'. From then on until the 1923 sale the house was occupied by a succession of huntsmen starting with William Griffiths.

The two names associated with the property, Saffrons Cross and Ketch, are both hard to interpret since no really early names have been found for the site. As regards the name 'Saffron' there is no evidence that either the wild Meadow Saffron, *Colchicum autumnale*, or the Saffron crocus, *Crocus sativus*, once grown for the dye obtained from it, have anything to do with the name as used here. The early spelling of 'Sevan Cross' might refer to a meeting of seven ways (see 80B). Before the enclosure act many roads were not hedged in and delimited as they are today and it may be that the area referred to as Sevan Cross was wider so that, in addition to the four roads that meet at the cross-roads here today, the name could have included a way from Riffins Mill, another from Lugg Mill (78) and the lane that joins the main road from the Isle of Rhea. This would make seven ways.

The alternative name 'Catch' or 'Ketch' is said to be to do with land on a boundary and certainly this house stands near the boundary between the Townships of Bodenham Devereux and Bowley.

The Ketch

The addition of 'Gate' to the name probably in this case, unlike most other 'Gate' names in Bodenham, refers to the Toll Gate associated with the Toll House which still stands on the opposite side of the road (in Bowley Township). This is born out by the fact that, although the manorial records are full of references to various gates into the open fields that needed repair, no Catch or Ketch Gate is mentioned nor was there an open field of that name.

(73) Greening Tree / Grinding Tree, Woodhouse Lane (B76 / Box 8 Bundle 42)

The present cottages were built c.1966 and replaced a single, older cottage built in the late seventeenth century. This was described in 1931 as being in good condition, of timber-frame construction (though the timbers were rather thin) and with a stone slate roof. The cottage was of two storeys the upstairs being probably reached by a ladder. There was a large, stone-built chimney at the west end and a lean-to of the same age as the house all along the back.

This was fairly certainly the cottage called Greening Tree that in 1680 was left by John Careles of the Woodhouse (75) to his sons John and Thomas. They probably sold it because by 1700 the cottage was owned and occupied by Richard Hegdon, a tailor who also occupied 1 acre in the nearby Inlands Field.

Richard Hegdon sold the cottage to Ann Flower who bequeathed it to her grandson Richard Symonds. He was a cooper and lived there with his wife Eleanor and left it to his grandson, Thomas Reynolds. By this time it was mortgaged to Thomas Hope, a weaver of Vicarage Cottages (34) and was described as: 'cottage, garden, orchard and fold at Greening Tree in a field called by the name of Heame'.

Thomas Hope transferred the mortgage in 1795 to Joseph Watkins, a shoemaker who lived at the Moor. He was an ardent non-conformist and built Bodenham's original chapel beside his house on the Moor. When he died he left his property to Trustees for the benefit of the chapel and they sold the Greening Tree to the Hampton Court estate in 1836 for £300.

Over all this period the constant presence of craftsmen of some sort; tailor, cooper, weaver, shoemaker, blacksmith, seems to imply some sort of workshop on the premises. But it was also a smallholding for it had a cidermill, pigsty and cowhouse. Then in 1868 the estate pulled down all the farm buildings, levelled the ground and 'made it suitable for a workman's cottage with a new pigsty and

Greening Tree, Woodhouse Lane

privy'. The land was taken from it and added to the big farm next door and the inhabitants afterwards were agricultural labourers, probably working at the Woodhouse Farm. In 1919 the cottage was sold as a part of that farm. From at least 1700 two names were in use for the property, Greening Tree and Grinding Tree—Grinding is said to be an alternative word for Greening. The Vicar, Rev H.C. Sturges, writing in his parish magazine around 1895, makes it clear that the tree in question was a large old oak which still stood beside the cottage at that time.

(74) Berkely Hill / Bartly Hill / Barclay Hill

This cottage, which was taken down in the late 1960s and not replaced, was built in the seventeenth century. It was timber-framed with a thatched roof and had one large, stone chimney. It was of two storeys with two communicating rooms downstairs, only one of which had a fire. The outhouse at one end was probably a wash-house since it had a chimney. These details come from a report and photograph made by the RCHM in 1931.

The earliest record found for this cottage is for 1710 when a William Davis 'of Bartley Hill' was in trouble with the Consistory Court of Hereford for 'taking away his fruit without paying tithe'. It must have been very frustrating to have to leave your fruit, perhaps exposed to the weather, until someone came to assess and remove the Rector or Vicar's tenth share and Davis had not waited.

The cottage was probably a part of the Woodhouse Farm (75) for a long time. Certainly 'Barclay Hill Coppice' was sold by the Marquis of Bath to the Earl of Essex in 1803 and the cottage probably came to the Arkwrights in 1810 along with the Woodhouse. It seems to have needed little repairing, the only work done being re-thatching in 1826.

Occupants included William and Elizabeth Lawrence in 1841, William Mason in 1851 and then apparently two families in 1861, those of William Billings and John Floyd, all the above being agricultural labourers. A succession of people lived there in the twentieth century, the last being a Mr Combs. Just why the cottage was demolished is not known, but probably because it was considered too isolated and lacking in modern facilities.

Berkeley Hill

(75) The Woodhouse / Woodhouse Farm

The house was built around 1600 on an L-shaped plan. The west wing was extended in the seventeenth century and there were more additions in the eighteenth century and later.

The property formed a part of the manor of Bodenham Devereux from early times and with it became a part of the Hampton Court estate in 1803. The name Woodhouse probably indicates that this westwards extension of the manor of Bodenham Devereux was originally made to incorporate the valuable woodlands on the hills around the farm into the manor.

The Carless family were early tenants of the farm and the will of John Carless 'of the Woodhouse' made in 1680 shows that he was a wealthy man. The inventory of his possessions includes luxuries like silver plate and a looking glass. Two 'chambers in the new building' are mentioned and in the barns as well as hay, wheat and rye, peas and pulses, he was storing flax and hemp.

Among subsequent tenants was William South whose household filled three pews in the church and Thomas Sirrell who was there when Richard Arkwright bought the estate. However the report on the farm made soon after in 1828 was not encouraging:

> The Woodhouse farm is in a wet inconvenient situation and with a very bad road occasioned by (the timber from) Tankard Walls and the Old Coppice woods being brought down the road to the homestead. Some repairs are wanted at the tiling of the new part of the house as the wet gets in. A shed roof where the servants sleep in the old part of the house wants stripping and new tiling ... some repairs are wanted at the tiling and boarding of the Upper Barn and pigsties.

All these farm buildings and more are shown on an 1834 plan of the farm yard.

Mr Hodges followed Thomas Sirrell as tenant and then Samuel Perkins and Daniel Brassington for whom a 'new pleasure ground' and 'a new road over Gt Pitt and Englands Fields' were made and 227 apple stocks planted. The latter were presumably grafted *in situ* the following year.

By the 1880s John and Elizabeth Knott were the tenants followed by John Samuel Knott who bought the farm in 1919. Later it was sold to Simon Romilly and so became a part of the Broadfield Court estate for the first time.

Woodhouse Farm

(76) Old Coppice

This cottage, which no longer stands, was built to house one of the Hampton Court estate game-keepers in 1859. It was built on a previously unoccupied site on the edge of the wood called Old Coppice above the Woodhouse (75) and was inhabited up to the First World War at least.

The massive stone jambs to the doorways stood six feet out of the ground and probably came from the nearby quarry at Dudales Hope. The lintels and sills of the windows were also made from single pieces of stone, carefully chamfered, but the internal walls were brick. Lower House in Bowley Lane, built in 1860 is said to be a larger version of this cottage. Water was provided by a well. A succession of gamekeepers lived here and in 1881 it was Elias Gaurd with his wife Honour who was a dressmaker.

(77) Dunfield Cottage

This cottage stood at the bottom of 'God-Almighty' hill on the north side of the road from Bodenham to Marden until about 1930. The level platform on which the house stood is still visible and it is remembered that it was a stone cottage with one chimney.

In 1804 Velters Morris paid pew rent for this cottage. Later this rent was paid by William Bennet who lived at Ashgrove Farm just above, which farm is actually in Marden rather than Bodenham parish. In earlier days it was called Coddy Meadow Farm and shares its name with the very steep hill out of Bodenham nearby. Today's name for this hill, given above, is a corruption of 'Coddy Meadow'.

Dunfield Cottage took its name from the former open arable field called Dunfield beside which it was built. Probably the last person to live in the cottage was a Mr Tong who also rented the 'Cuckoo Patch', a small field on the slope above.

(78) Old Lugg Mill / Lugg Mill / Lugg & Scut Mill / Box & Scut Mill

Today all memory of this mill has gone except for the name Millcroft. The farm of this name (62) was called after the former open arable field, Millcroft Field, and this in turn must have taken its name from the Mill itself which stood beside the River Lugg nearby (see section on the open fields, 83).

Mills, if present, were recorded in Domesday Book and in Bodenham a mill was listed but it stood in the part of the parish that later became the Moor Township. As the River Lugg does not flow through this area it seems that Lugg Mill must have been built after Domesday, but probably not much later for a mill was a vital part of the village economy. The mill normally belonged to the lord of the manor and Lugg Mill certainly belonged to the Devereux family in 1611 when the Earl of Essex (Devereux) leased out 'two mills Box and Scutt' to Thomas Vicar of London with the Woodhouse (75). (The term 'two mills' probably meant two wheels or two sets of stones and not two mill buildings.) The 'Scutt Mill' may have been concerned with dressing hemp or flax but it is not known what the 'Box mill' did. Three other leases were to do with 'the wayes to Lugg and Scutt Mill' for which the rent was 3s 4d or a sparrow hawk.

After this the Mill was just known as Lugg Mill and was rented to a succession of people. One of these was William Gibbons. He died in 1684 and his will and inventory have survived. The latter shows that the house in which he lived was a part of the mill building. The house consisted of three rooms: 'the dwelling room, the chamber over the dwelling room and the chamber over the mill'. Each room had a bed in it but rather little else. William Gibbons had three horses and eight swine but apparently no cattle or sheep which was unusual in Bodenham. The horses were probably for carting corn and flour and the swine may have been kept to feed on spilt or damaged grain. After William Gibbons' death his widow remained at the mill for a few years but then in 1698 disaster struck—not storms or floods but a man-made disaster that swept away all the mills on the lower reaches of the Wye and the Lugg.

There had always been conflict on rivers between mill owners, who required weirs across the river to provide the power needed to turn the mill wheel, and those whose business was with boats for whom weirs were nothing but an obstruction. This was a conflict that was not really resolved until the invention of the pound lock. However towards the end of the seventeenth century there was a lot of talk about improving navigation on the lower Wye and Lugg and in 1695 an Act of Parliament was passed setting up commissioners empowered to buy up all the mills on the two rivers and destroy them thus letting the rivers run free of the restricting weirs. Despite a lot of opposition the plan was actually carried out. In preparation for this a survey was made to find where all the mills were situated and what their value was. In 1697 the surveyor reported for Bodenham that: 'About a mile below Hampton Court are two mills belonging to Lord Viscount Weymouth [a Devereux] let now ... at £11- 10s per annum'. Then in 1698 in the navigation accounts comes the entry: 'paid Mr John Hill for taking down Lord Weymouth's weir upon Lugg £2. 10s 0d'.

Without the weir the mill could no longer function, but though no longer grinding corn the mill building and its land continued to appear in rentals and in 1777 and 1798 were being let to Mr South under the name of 'Old Lugg Mill' together with 'Corbetts Farm' (31).

After this no more is heard of Lugg Mill but although the written records cease evidence on the ground remains to this day. 'Just about a mile below Hampton Court', as described by the seventeenth-century surveyor, near to the place where Riffins Brook joins the river, the weir can still be seen. It is made of well cut stone and stands up out of the water when the river is low. There is a gap against the right bank and Mr Derek Knott recalls how, when hops were grown on the slopes of Bunhill, planks used to be placed across this gap so that people living in Bowley Lane could cross the river here to work in the hop yard thus saving a long walk round by the bridge.

The gap does not however seem large enough to be the breach made in 1698 to allow boats to pass and is more probably the result of natural erosion. If that is so then the breech must have been by the left bank. Here there is today a large pile of jumbled stone, some dressed and all covered in vegetation. A possible explanation of this stonework is that the breach was made here and that subsequently in the early eighteenth century it was replaced by a lock of which the stones are the remains. Locks were certainly made on the Lugg at this time in at least eight places, one being at Hampton Court where the lock chamber can still be seen.

The building of these locks was an attempt by Leominster Council, acting on its own, to make the Lugg navigable. This navigation was not really successful but one notable cargo to pass down the river all the way from Leominster to Chepstow and back up again was the six bells from the Priory. These went down the river to be recast and made into eight bells which then returned up the river. The bills for this transaction remain but no one seems to have noted this unusual cargo going past.

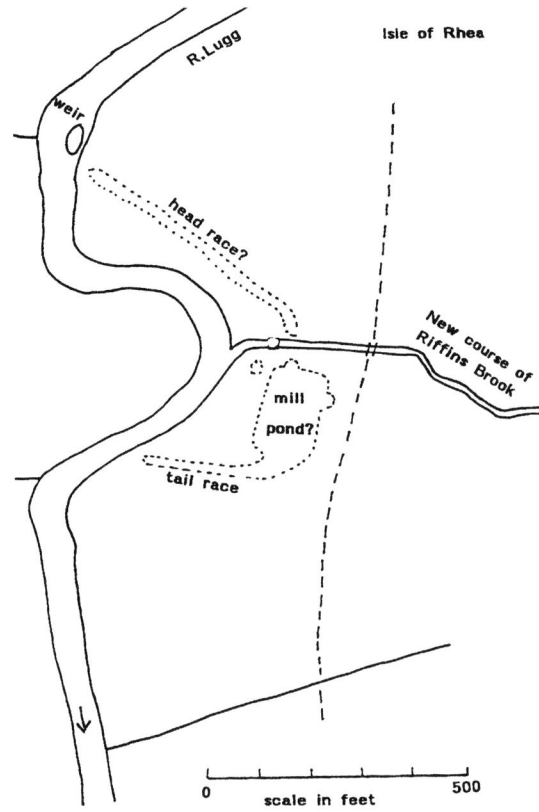

R. Lugg
Isle of Rhea
weir
head race?
New course of Riffins Brook
mill pond?
tail race
0   scale in feet   500

The position of the mill itself as opposed to the weir is not so certain but it seems unlikely that the wheel was actually in the river because the Lugg sometimes rises very rapidly and a mill so close to the river would be in danger of being swept away in times of flood, taking with it perhaps someone asleep in the 'chamber over the wheel'. The diagram shows an alternative arrangement. The suggested head-race is still today a very distinct channel in the ground and the weir would have diverted water down this to a mill pond beside which the mill would have stood. A large, squarish depression in the field today could well have been this pond.

However as things stand today this arrangement would not have worked because Riffins Brook cuts across the suggested head-race. But at the time the mill was functioning Riffins Brook took another course, flowing south to join Millcroft Brook before entering the Lugg. A new channel was cut for the brook, probably in the nineteenth century, to lessen flooding in the Millcroft area.

(79) The Pound

The Pound had an important role to play in the village economy in pre-enclosure days and was in use in Bodenham for the impounding of stray animals up to the nineteenth century.

All that remains today of the original square stone structure are two low walls set at right angles to each other, one is beside the road and the other divides the gardens of 'Welton' and what used to be called 'Pound Cottage' (42). But within living memory the Pound had all four walls standing with a locked gate on the roadside. The stones were gradually removed and the ground incorporated into gardens. When the name of Pound Cottage was changed to 'Rainbow' recently the last remembrance of this once important part of village life disappeared.

Before it fell into decay the Bodenham pound probably looked very like the one still standing by Canon Pyon church. It seems that it was originally free-standing in an open space later taken over by gardens (see 44).

The pound was the responsibility of the lord of the manor and from 1687 at least his steward was frequently asked to see to its repair. In 1789 a new 'doorcase and gate' were made by William Gladding (see 36), who paid the Blacksmith '2 shillings for hooks and eyes, hasp and staples'. In 1815 it was said to have been 'rebuilt'. At that time Thomas Wright (see 41) was the 'Bodenham impounder'.

In 1722 there was a serious affray at the Pound which ended in a court case. Two of Lord Coningsby's bailiffs had taken three cows and two oxen from the 'Upper Vern' farm in lieu of arrears of rent and put them in the Bodenham Pound. While 'the bailiffs were attending to the animals about 20 men came up pretending they had a warrant from the sheriff'. They took an iron crowbar and axe and broke open the pound, drove the cattle out and carried off the bailiffs as prisoners threatening them, 'hollowing and shooting, whereby they were in danger of their lives'. This went on all one Saturday and Sunday and how it ended is not clear but it is the nearest thing to a riot that has been noted in the Bodenham records.

(80) The Bridges

80 (A) Bodenham Bridge

There has probably been an important crossing of the River Lugg at this point for a very long time. The track along the top of Dinmore Hill from the west comes down the slope of Bunhill and leads to the bridge. This path down the hill lies in a hollow way cut deeply into the ground by long passage of people and animals. In early days the crossing was presumably a ford and flat stones are sometimes visible just below the bridge when the water is clear. The right of way down to the river's edge between the bridge and the smithy (45), that serves as a drinking place for animals and is also used for launching boats, was probably the original way down to the ford and the roadside still widens here as it approaches the river.

When the first bridge replaced the ford we do not know but in the seventeenth century there was a low, stone bridge here, standing slightly downstream of the present bridge. A raised causeway can be seen in the field to the east that led towards it and in 1957 when some works were going on in the bed of the river the bases of two bridge piers were exposed here (information from Mr Trevor Barra) which means that it was a three arched bridge. It was maintained at the expense of the County and as a result information on the condition of the bridge was recorded in the Quarter Sessions records. In 1672 it was said to be 'in decay' and in 1695 £25 was spent on repairs.

In 1697 a survey of mills and other obstructions on the river was made in connection with the 1697 Navigation Act (see 78) and of Bodenham the surveyor reported: 'next is Bodnam Bridge, built of stone but very low must have one arch raised'.

Though the navigation accounts have rather little else to say about Bodenham, judging from what happened to other bridges over the Lugg, it seems probable that, rather than raising the central arch in stone at considerable expense, they just broke the arch and put planks or a rudimentary sort of drawbridge across the gap. This was certainly done at both Marden and Lugwardine and led to complaints that the planks were missing or that the draw-bridge was unsafe so that people dare not cross over. In the end Marden got a new central arch of brick and Lugwardine got a whole new bridge. By 1717 Bodenham bridge was 'growing much out of repair and if not speedily attended to will be in a little time a great expense'. This time £10 was allocated but only half of that amount was spent.

Never the less the Bridge kept going until 1799 when John Gethin of Kingsland, known as the 'Bridge Builder', was directed to survey all the county bridges. His report for Bodenham Bridge must have been bad for he went on to produce plans for a new bridge and for a new Five-footed Bridge as well, the former estimated at £650 and the latter at £98. The plans were accepted and Richard Reynolds, Bodenham's Parish Clerk, wrote on the inside cover of his account book: 'Anno Dom.

1816 Bodenham New Bridge over the River Lugg and the Five-footed Bridge over the Moors Brook were built'.

The new bridge was designed with a single arch and circular holes in the spandrels. This design had become popular after such a bridge was built successfully over the River Taff at Pontypridd. That bridge, the longest arch in Britain for many years, incorporated such holes in the spandrels their purpose being to strengthen the arch by achieving a better distribution of weight and not to provide a relief channel for water. Up to the 1980s over 30 pairs of house martins built their nests each year on the south face of the bridge.

80 (B) The Five-Footed Bridge

This small bridge crosses the Moors Brook about 100 yards east of Bodenham Bridge, just before the brook joins the river. It was rebuilt in 1816 at the same time as Bodenham Bridge. Its unusual name was well known to the older inhabitants of the village and has been found in records back to the seventeenth century. At that time there were also references to the 'Five-footed cross' from which the bridge probably took its name. The 'Five-footed cross' was probably so called because it was a meeting place of five footways and still today five ways meet here:

a) the road to Bodenham bridge and on to the village and the church. Money was left by David Clark in his will in 1546 to 'make up' this stretch of road with stone.

b) Smeadall lane leading to Smeadall meadow, the fields beyond, and on to Marden.

c) Millcroft lane leading to Englands Gate with Ketch lane branching off leading to Bowley.

d) The way to Bodenham Mill (78) now the footpath beside the river.

e) The way to the Moor, now a footpath to Orchard Close. This crosses marshy ground and at one time was paved, some large flat stones still remain. This 'causeway' was mentioned in 1657 and in 1715 widow Hill was ordered 'to lay stepping stones in the causeway in Elmfield'.

80 (C) The Church Foot bridge / Byfield Bridge

There must always have been a river crossing of some sort near this place since several footpaths from distant parts of the parish meet here to cross to the church but the earliest crossing may well have been a ford. Certainly there are structures made of stones set on edge across the river bed at two places just below the present bridge. These have been sadly damaged in recent years by canoeists.

The Survey of 1697 (see 78) does not mention a bridge here but this might only mean that such a bridge was sufficiently high as to be no obstruction to boats. The earliest record found is for 1722 when a bridge here was called Byfield bridge after the field nearby.

Then in 1816 the Quarter Sessions record: 'Wooden bridge at Bodenham, clerk to contact Mr Gethin to build this bridge at £28'. This note probably referred to the church bridge and an early photo, taken before 1890 shows a wooden bridge—'a rustic affair' as Mrs Pound of the Old Post Office (9) remembered it. The fact that the bridge was a county responsibility indicates its importance and perhaps its age. The 'rustic' bridge was replaced by a metal one before the First World War and that by another metal bridge in 1972. Both of these later bridges had a metal turnstile at the left bank end on which generations of small children delighted in twirling around. This was summarily removed by the council in 2001 but replaced nearby by the residents the following year.

80 (D) Bendbridge / Benbridge

This is the bridge over Riffins Brook in Ketch Lane. The earliest mention found is in 1689 when it was called 'Bendbridge'. In 1813 it was called 'Benbridge'.

80 (E) Other Bridges

There are several smaller bridges in the Township. Two of those described below seem to have been associated with the irrigation of water meadows and two are of interest for their simple structure.

a) A bridge near Dinmore crosses the stream flowing from the waterfall just before it enters the river. This stream has obviously been diverted to flow close under the hill for quite a distance before turning towards the river. It may have been associated with irrigation of water meadows here in the nineteenth century because there are grooves on either side of the bridge supports where boards could have been slotted to control the water level. In the past it would have carried the old West Lane (see section on roads). Hampton Court employed 'a drowner' in the nineteenth century whose job involved the management of the flood-plain meadows beside the River Lugg as water meadows. These were irrigated by water from side streams diverted at will to flow over the meadows providing an early bite of grass in spring.

b) There is a concrete bridge on the footpath to the Vern which must also have been associated with the irrigation of water meadows because the sluice gear is still present.

c) Another footbridge on the path leading to the Vern is of interest because it is made of one large slab of stone, reminiscent of the clapper bridges of Dartmoor.

d) There is a similar 'clapper bridge' crossing a stream just on the church side of Church bridge.

(81) The Village Green, Cross Well, Market cross and War Memorial

The village green is a small, grassy triangle that lies at the junction of four old roads, the West Lane (see 21), Ladywell Lane, the road to the Bridge and the road to the Church. This is really the centre of the village and any consideration of the Green itself, which was probably formerly much larger, might take us back to the origins of the settlement which is well beyond the scope of this booklet. However the three structures standing there today, the Cross Well, the socket stone of the Market Cross and the War Memorial, all have an important place in Bodenham's more recent history.

The earliest reference to the Cross yet found was in 1690 when the inhabitants of the Township were to be fined 'if they do not keep the spring or stream leading from the Cross to the River Lugg on its right course'. The spring still flows, running now from the circular stone structure known as the Cross Well but from thence now underground. The water that emerges is quite warm and where it flows in a pipe under the road in times of frost and snow melts a line on the road above it (this water does not come from the spring in Ladywell Lane).

In earlier times the spring fed a pond on the Green which was used as a drinking place, for farm animals. Presumably there was some separate arrangement for people collecting drinking water. In 1876 this situation was declared insanitary and the surveyor, Thomas Landon, who lived at Hill House (54), had the spring enclosed in the present structure with pipes emerging at various heights up the side. The water used to emerge from the top pipe but for many years now it has never been as high. There was a story that when mains water was brought to the village the supply to the Cross Well was restricted in some way to encourage householders to go on the mains.

In 1378 a grant was made to Walter Devereux to hold a weekly market in Bodenham and the socket stone for the market cross, which still stands on the Green today, dates from that period. It seems, however, that the market was never very successful, perhaps because it was too near the existing markets at Hereford and Leominster.

Never-the-less there are unauthenticated stories that Bodenham once had a market house on the Green, similar to that at Pembridge where one of the corner posts rests on a socket stone very like the Bodenham stone. Be that as it may trading of a sort certainly went on here at the end of the eighteenth century for Mrs Reynolds of Cross Well cottage (30), who was born in 1833, remembered her parents-in-law, who had lived in the cottage before her, describing how women used to bring their market baskets to the Green and place them on the large stones that lay around there at that time. (Some of these were probably the ancient carved stones that became incorporated into a rockery in the garden of the Hollies (19) and were recently taken to the church.)

The upright stone in the ancient socket is of much later date and came from the quarry at Dudales Hope (see 27). It was only erected in the 1840s and at that time was very much taller, narrowing at the top to a point. It was known as 'the pinnacle' by the children who played around it.

The third structure on the Green, the War Memorial, was erected in 1921 and dedicated in March of that year in pouring rain. The occasion was notable because it was only the second occasion in the country when the famous Armistice hymn 'Oh valiant hearts' was sung to its now traditional tune. The hymn was written by Sir John S. Arkwright of Hampton Court and the tune by Dr Harris of Colwall, the two men having been brought together by the vicar of Bodenham.

In earlier times there was probably another structure here, the Village Stocks. In 1690 this was out of repair and Thomas Hill of the Cross Farm (19) was ordered to mend them. As his farm was beside the Green it seems likely that the stocks too were on the Green. In 1796 new stocks and also a new Whipping Post were made.

The licence for a weekly market granted in 1378 also included permission to hold an annual fair on the Feast of the Assumption (15th of August) and the two days on either side. The date is significant as fairs were normally held on the day of the patron saint of the church and this confirms that Bodenham church was dedicated to the Virgin Mary at that date. No evidence of a fair ever taking place has been discovered but the site, with the Village Green leading down to Peasegreen, is ideal for such an event (and the royal permission is still probably valid should the village wish to resurrect it !).

The Pinnacle and fourteenth-century socket stone

(82) The Lady Well

This spring, which is situated up Ladywell Lane, still provides a constant supply of good water and its presence, together with that of the Cross Well on the Green, may well have led to the establishment of the original settlement at this place. This spring was named after the Virgin Mary to whom Bodenham church was originally dedicated. The use of the archaic form of the possessive case, 'Lady Well' rather than the modern form, 'Ladies Well' indicates the age of the name. It was described in the past as a 'proper spring with an arch over it' and the families at the cottages up the lane above got their water from there.

The Hampton Court estate piped water from this spring to their properties in the village and as these all came to use more and more water the supply was augmented sometime between 1887 and 1904 by piping water along the side of the hill from the waterfall spring (see 54) to a structure just above the Lady Well. The first, 1887, edition of the 25 inch O.S. map marks the position of the true Lady Well but the second, 1904 edition, marks only the structure above described as 'well'.

At one time water rents were paid to the estate and the water was tested regularly by the local authority who took a sample from a standpipe near the church. (The overflow from the spring is piped down beside the lane, under the road and on towards the gravel pits and has nothing to do with the Cross Well.)

The water from the Ladywell is very hard and bits of tufa have been found in the soil around. The lane leading up to the spring is sunk in a deep linear depression which widens out into a circular depression around the spring itself. This could indicate that here, as at the waterfall, there was once a large deposit of tufa. If so this might well have been the source of the tufa of which Bodenham's Norman church was built.

(83) The Roads through the village

During the nineteenth century the pattern of roads in the Township west of the river bridge was considerably altered but in most places the course of the earlier roads can still be traced on the ground. The changes resulted from two major events in the village the first being the Enclosure Act of 1813 and the second the building of Rev Henry Arkwright's new vicarage (55).

Before the Enclosure Act two roads led west from the bridge, one to the Cross Well and Green the other diverging from this to climb the slope of the hill to the Henhouse (53) and on westwards. Where these two roads diverged there was a triangle of land on which stood 'the village elm'. (This tree probably went well before the advent of elm disease.)

At the Cross Well then as now four roads met but although the roads south to the church and east to the bridge were still as they are today the other two are not. The road north Ladywell Lane, still follows the same course today as in the past, but whereas it was formerly of equal importance to the other roads today it is just a grassy track. The other road, that to the west called the West Lane, has gone completely. This road ran along the bottom of the valley and its former course is still indicated by the line of the wall beside the road bounding the Hollies (19) which at first follows the road but then curves away from it. Where the wall ends the line of the old West Lane is continued by a depression crossing the field and then running along the fence line between the gravel pit car park and the orchard until it now ends in a lake. Before this gravel pit was dug

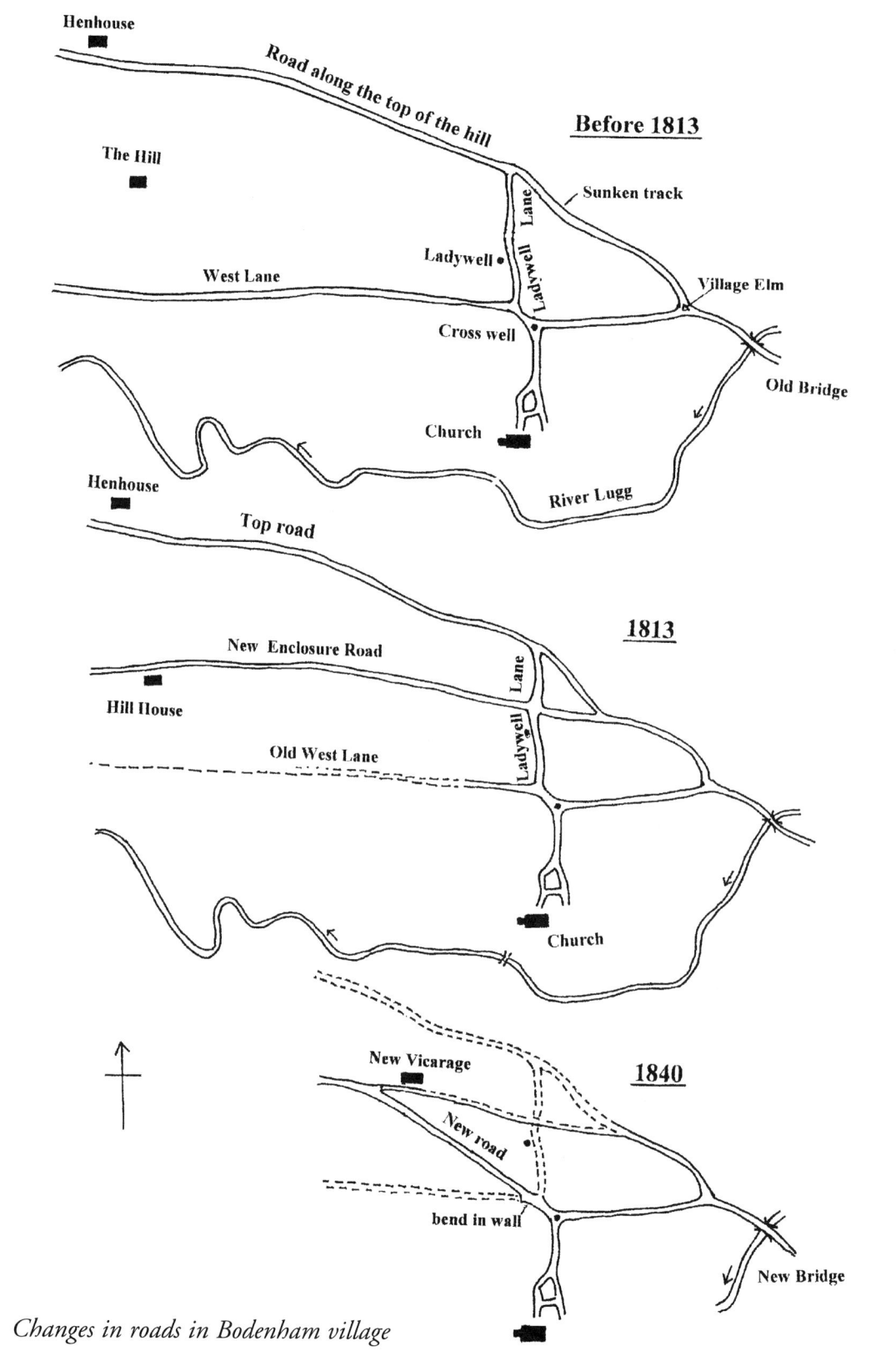

Henhouse

Road along the top of the hill

Before 1813

The Hill

Sunken track

Ladywell Lane

Ladywell

West Lane

Village Elm

Cross well

Old Bridge

Church

Henhouse

River Lugg

Top road

1813

New Enclosure Road

Ladywell Lane

Hill House

Old West Lane

Ladywell

Church

New Vicarage

1840

New road

bend in wall

New Bridge

Changes in roads in Bodenham village

the hedges on both sides of the former lane were still present and Ladyclose Farm (21) fronted onto it.

As a result of the Enclosure Act of 1813 a new west road was built along the side of the hill and this, from the drive gates of Bodenham Manor (55) westwards, is the road we have today. But the eastern end of this enclosure road has all but gone. It started between the Old Vicarage (39) and Bank House (41) at the 'village elm'. From here it first followed the old track leading up to Dinmore hill. But where today this track comes into the open field and the way to the top carries on upwards the enclosure road led off to the left and can still be seen as a level, slightly flattened track which runs along the side of the hill, first at the edge of the field, then just above the Hampton Court orchard and then along the line of the Bodenham Manor drive to where this joins the road and so on to Dinmore where it is still the road in use today.

The building of this enclosure road had a devastating effect on Ladywell Lane which, because it lay in a deep depression was in the way. As a result it was officially closed and the depression was filled in to carry the new road level across the top. This left a very steep bank on the south side completely blocking the lane. The steep bank is still there today and has recently had steps made up its face.

All this was done despite the two inhabited cottages beside the lane above the place where the enclosure road crossed it. The inhabitants of these cottages relied on the Lady well for their water and after the enclosure road was made they had somehow to carry buckets up and down the steep slope. It is no wonder that in due course the cottages became uninhabited.

In 1844 these roads were changed again because the site chosen for the new Vicarage (55) was right on top of the recently built enclosure road. As a result the whole western end of that road was closed officially and because this closure would have left the village with no way out to the west (since the old West Lane had by now gone out of use) a new length of road was built running from the Cross Well to join the remaining part of the enclosure road by the westward gate into Bodenham Manor. This is the stretch of road in use today. It was built by large numbers of Hampton Court estate workers equipped with numerous wheelbarrows which, according to the estate accounts, were continually breaking down.

(84) Notes on the open arable fields

Although this booklet has been concerned with the houses of the Township there has inevitably been mention of the land that was associated with those houses and this often included arable in the open fields. So it is perhaps necessary to give a brief account of these fields and of farming in Bodenham before the Enclosure Act of 1813.

Over most of central England from medieval times on 'open field' agriculture prevailed as a part of the manorial system. The five main elements of this system were:

1) arable land—organised in large 'open fields' each divided into many long, narrow strips known as 'ridges'. These were cultivated by different people but in any one field they all grew the same crop in any one year.

2) meadow—lying on the most fertile land by river or stream where hay to feed the plough oxen through the winter was grown. Here too each man had one or more strips but after hay-making

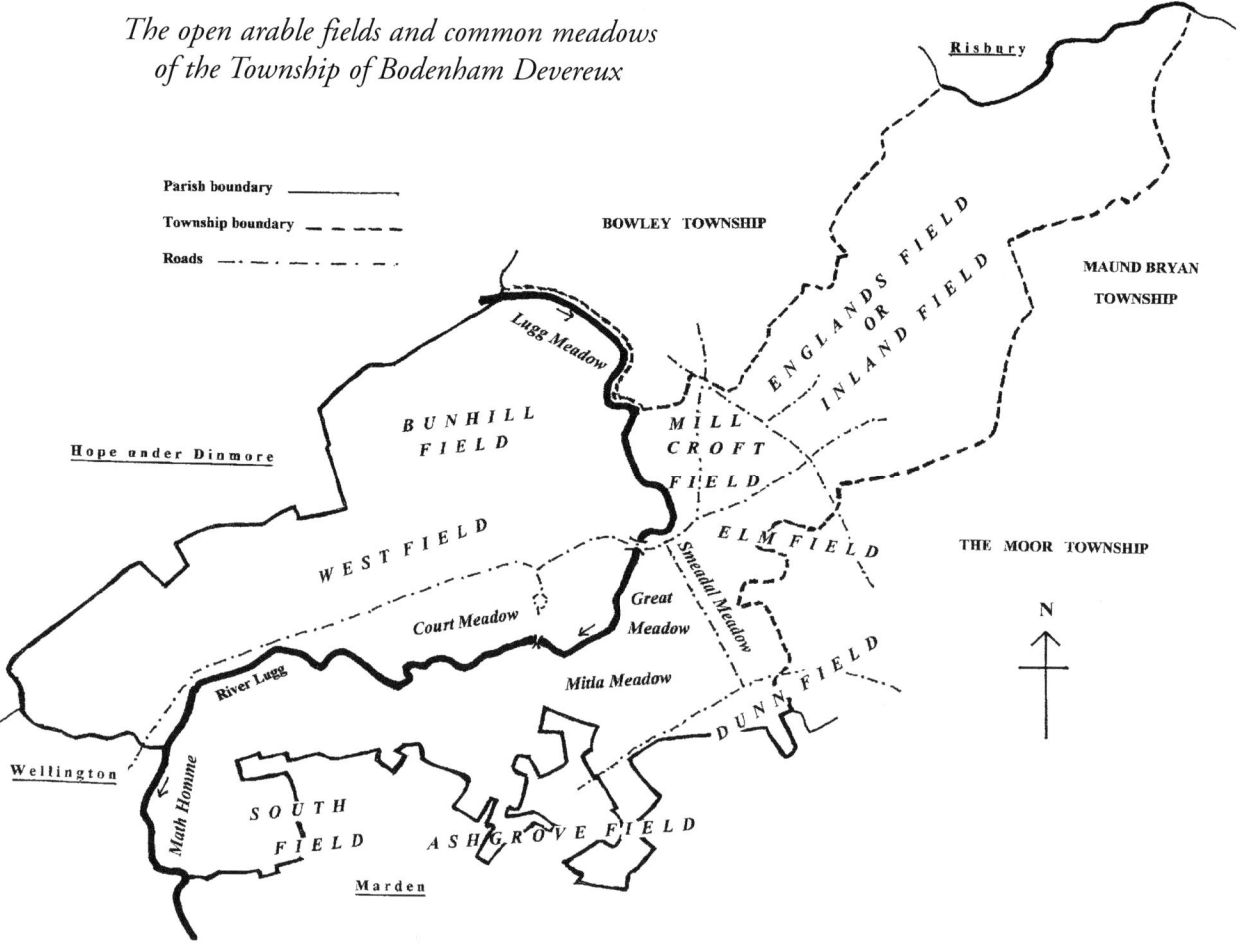

The open arable fields and common meadows of the Township of Bodenham Devereux

Parish boundary ————————
Township boundary — — — — —
Roads —·—·—·—·—·—

BOWLEY TOWNSHIP

Risbury

MAUND BRYAN TOWNSHIP

Lugg Meadow

BUNHILL FIELD

Hope under Dinmore

ENGLANDS FIELD OR INLAND FIELD

MILL CROFT FIELD

WEST FIELD

ELM FIELD

THE MOOR TOWNSHIP

Court Meadow

Great Meadow

Smeadal Meadow

N

Mitla Meadow

River Lugg

DUNN FIELD

Wellington

Math Homme

SOUTH FIELD

ASH GROVE FIELD

Marden

the whole meadow was thrown open for communal grazing from Lammas day (August 1st) until the following Candlemas (Feb. 2nd). Meadowland was always valued much more highly than any other type of land in the parish.

3) woodland— usually on the edge of the parish or on slopes too steep for agriculture. Most was coppiced to provide fagots for burning and wood for wattle, poles etc but some trees were allowed to grow to full height to provide timber for building.

4) the manorial waste—poorer land, often on the edge of the parish which provided useful, rough grazing at all times of year but the manorial waste could also include the village green.

5) the manorial court—which was held twice a year at the lord of the manor's house known as the 'Court' in Herefordshire for this reason. This court controlled the whole system and fined those who committed offences or did not conform. It was presided over normally by the Lord of the Manor's steward.

This system either never really existed or broke down very early along the Welsh Border and most parishes in the west of Herefordshire show rather little evidence of former open fields. But in central Herefordshire the system was well established in parishes in the lower Lugg valley and was not finally extinguished in Bodenham until 1813. It differed here however from the central counties of England in that instead of having just three large open fields there were four or more smaller ones and in Bodenham parish each Township had its own open fields.

In the Township of Bodenham Devereux the various elements of the system can be deduced from the enclosure map and from old deeds:

a) arable land—there were at least five open fields, West Field, Bunhill Field, Millcroft Field, Englands or Inland Field and Elm Field. Some of these names were recorded in the fourteenth century. In addition Ashgrove Field and South Field were shared with Marden parish, hence the jagged parish boundary in this area with frequent right-angled bends. In places strips owned by Bodenham were entirely surrounded by Marden parish and visa versa. Clearly here the open field boundaries pre-dated the parish boundary. Each field would have had its own hedge and gate or gates leading into it. Houses that held land in one of the open fields are likely to be older, or stand on an older site than houses that did not.

b) meadow—the Township was particularly rich in meadow land which lay beside the Lugg on the low-lying land that flooded regularly. These common meadows were called Smeadal, Mitley, the Homme, Lugg Meadow, Court Meadow and Math Homme.

c) woodland—this was and still is situated on steep slopes in two parts of the Township, Dinmore Hill and above the Woodhouse Farm (75). These woods all give evidence of formerly being coppiced and have the flora associated with 'ancient woodland'.

d) manorial waste—the township was probably short of manorial waste but evidence from a number of houses near the church and up to the Cross Well seems to indicate that the area known as 'Peasegreen', which may have formerly been quite large, was considered to be manorial waste. Only one of the houses in this area had land in the open fields instead they tended to be occupied by craftsman and small traders rather than farmers.

e) the manorial court—this was held at Devereux Court (20) and was presided over by the lord of the manor's steward who lived in the house and kept the Court records, at first on rolls of parchment and later in books—many of these have survived.

Index of Family Names

The numbers given represent the number allocated to the property in the previous pages, not the page numbers themselves